Praise for Guitar H

CW01475831

A Stellar Writing

"The Guitar Head books have been an invaluable resource, helping me fulfill a lifetime dream of mastering guitar soloing. It's my retirement plan! Keep the books coming, as I just can't get enough! Thank you so much for your stellar writing and loving approach to the guitar — it really resonates with me."

- *Stephen E. Dannenbaum*

50's Mid-Life Guitar Start up

"Starting up guitar for myself in my late 50's after sending all my kids thru guitar school, Really great books, I have purchased them all. Very helpful to fill in the blanks. Easy to follow and I really enjoy his writing style and humor"

- *Wayne Humphrey*

Exceeded Expectations

"Guitar fretboard is the first book I bought from Guitar Head. I purchased this book with much skepticism. However my skepticism quickly went away. I am an online student with Berklee College of Music and can tell you their books are real deal. Looking forward to purchasing the complete series of books from Guitar Head."

- *Steven Retalic*

Great hints and tips

"Guitar Head allowed me to view the fretboard entirely differently than I have for over 50 YEARS! Thank You Guitar Head!"

- *Kim Gregg*

BLUES GUITAR FOR NOOBS

How to get
your basics right
so you can finally
crack blues music

GUITAR HEAD

GH@theguitarhead.com
facebook.com/theguitarhead
instagram.com/theguitarhead

©Copyright 2021 by Guitar Head - All rights reserved.

This document is geared towards providing exact and reliable information in regard to the topic and issue covered. The publication is sold with the idea that the publisher is not required to render accounting, officially permitted, or otherwise, qualified services. If advice is necessary, legal or professional, a practiced individual in the profession should be ordered.

- From a Declaration of Principles which was accepted and approved equally by a Committee of the American Bar Association and a Committee of Publishers and Associations.

In no way is it legal to reproduce, duplicate, or transmit any part of this document in either electronic means or in printed format. Recording of this publication is strictly prohibited and any storage of this document is not allowed unless with written permission from the publisher. All rights reserved.

The information provided herein is stated to be truthful and consistent, in that any liability, in terms of inattention or otherwise, by any usage or abuse of any policies, processes, or directions contained within is the solitary and utter responsibility of the recipient reader. Under no circumstances will any legal responsibility or blame be held against the publisher for any reparation, damages, or monetary loss due to the information herein, either directly or indirectly.

Respective authors own all copyrights not held by the publisher.

The information herein is offered for informational purposes solely and is universal as so. The presentation of the information is without contract or any type of guaranteed assurance.

The trademarks that are used are without any consent, and the publication of the trademark is without permission or backing by the trademark owner. All trademarks and brands within this book are for clarifying purposes only and are the owned by the owners themselves, not affiliated with this document.

Disclaimer

Please note the information contained within this document is for educational and entertainment purposes only. Every attempt has been made to provide accurate, up to date and reliable complete information. No warranties of any kind are expressed or implied. Readers acknowledge that the author is not engaging in the rendering of legal and financial, medical or professional advice. The content of this book has been derived from various sources. Please consult a licensed professional before attempting any techniques outline in this book.

By reading this document, the reader agrees that under no circumstances are is the author responsible for any losses, direct or indirect, which are incurred as a result of the use of information contained within this document, including, but not limited to, - errors, omissions, or inaccuracies.

Dedication

---

*We dedicate this book to the complete
Guitar Head team,
supporters, well-wishers and
the Guitar Head community.*

*It goes without saying that we
would not have gotten
this far without
your encouragement,
critique and support*

Table Of Contents

Free Guitar Head Bonuses

Audio Files

All Guitar Head books come with audio tracks for the licks inside the book. These audio tracks are an integral part of the book - they ensure you are playing the charts and chords the way they are intended to be played.

Lifetime access to Guitar Head Community

Being around like-minded people is the first step to being successful at anything. The Guitar Head community is a place where you can find people who are willing to listen to your music, answer your questions or talk anything guitar.

Email Newsletters Sent Directly to Your Inbox

We send regular guitar lessons and tips to all our subscribers. Our subscribers are also the first to know about Guitar Head giveaways and holiday discounts.

Backing Tracks

This book comes with full - band backing tracks that you can use to practice your soloing! It'll also help your solos sound fuller and more musical.

Free PDF

Guitar mastery is all about the details! Getting the small things right and avoiding mistakes that can slow your guitar journey by years. So, we wrote a book about 25 of the most common mistakes guitarists make and decided to give it for free to all Guitar Head readers.

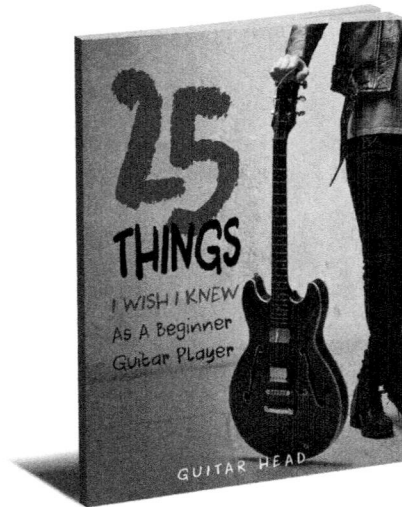

You can grab a copy of the free book, the audio files and subscribe to the newsletter by following the link below.

All these bonuses are a 100% free, with no strings attached. You won't need to enter any personal details other than your first name and email address.

To get your bonuses, go to: ***www.theguitarhead.com/bonus***

Book Profile

Difficulty Level: Intermediate

Technical knowledge you need before reading this book:

This book will teach you everything you need to start your blues journey on the right note. It's been geared towards a guitarist who is a noob at blues music. But we won't be covering "Guitar Basics" here to keep the book true to its intent. The following skills are recommended before you tackle this book:

- Fretboard knowledge.
- Scales in different keys.
- Knowledge of Chords and Chord progressions.
- Basic knowledge of techniques such as bends, vibrato, slides etc.

Suggested reading before this book:

The *Guitar Scales for Beginners* is a full-sized book teaching you just one scale! It'll handhold you through everything you need to know to play guitar scales even if you don't know what a scale is. You can find it on our website.

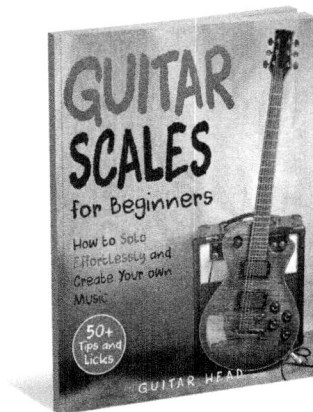

Note: Advanced guitar tab notation included at the end of the book.

Guitar Tablature
What It Is and How to Use It

-Feel free to skip, if you already know how to read tabs

Let's clear up something right from the start:

In order to master the guitar, you do NOT have to learn how to read music.

Yep. That's right. There are lots of famous guitarists that do not know how to read formal music. These include The Beatles, Eric Clapton, and Eddie Van Halen. However, I am not saying that learning to read music is a bad thing - quite the contrary. But it is true that you may well be able to reach your guitar-playing goals without needing to learn how to read countless pages of black lines with what looks like squashed ants all over the page.

To make things easier, in fact, MUCH easier, let's talk about an alternative way of noting (no pun intended) how to play the guitar. It's called "guitar tablature", or "tab" for short. It is similar to formal sheet music but it is far easier to understand, especially for beginner guitarists.

It looks like this (and by the way, this is a very famous melody!):

The top section shows formal music notation. But there is no need to concern yourself with that for now; in fact, you will often see guitar tab, where the music notation isn't there at all. However, it is very useful to have if you ever decide to take on learning how to read proper sheet music.

OK, now that's covered, let's take a good look at the lower section - the one that says "TAB" on it. You'll see that there are six lines that run horizontally across the page. Each of these lines represents one string of your guitar, with the line at the bottom representing the 6th string, and the line at the top representing the 1st string. Simple enough, right?

Therefore, when the guitar is on your lap, the string closest to you on the guitar (the 6th or Low (Thickest) E string) is the line closest to you on the TAB. And the string furthest from you on the guitar (the 1st or High (Thinnest) E string) is the line furthest away from you on the TAB. Some people do find this confusing at first, but it gets very easy, in a short amount of time with a little practice.

The numbers represent the frets that you are supposed to play the notes on. Even more simple!

There are other elements of reading tab that are similar to music notation, such as time signatures and measures. No need to go into that now - let's just concentrate on getting the notes right first.

So, let's check it out the tab again:

If you read the tab correctly, you'll play the following notes one after the other..

- 4th string — 2nd fret (index)
- 4th string — 2nd fret (index)
- 4th string — 4th fret (ring)
- 4th string — 2nd fret (index)
- 3rd string — 2nd fret (index)
- 3rd string — 1st fret (index)

Now that you've played it does it ring a bell? Sounds like "Happy Birthday" to me - and it will to you too after you get it down pat!

If you want to get deeper into the world of tabs, we have a whole book dedicated to reading tabs. It will teach you everything you need to know about reading tabs and comes with a vast dictionary of guitar notation symbols.

And what's better – it's free!

You can get the free pdf here: www.theguitarhead.com/tabs

Introduction

There are not too many styles of music with a more distinctive sound than the blues. The idiosyncrasies of this style can be found in every possible segment of the composition, performance and lyrical content itself. The characteristic chord progressions such as the 12-bar blues, the blues scale with the mandatory spice known as a "blue note," the shuffling rhythm and the lyrics that depict the cry for freedom of the enslaved African Americans in the Deep South of the USA are just some of the constituent elements that make blues so recognizable and loved by millions of people.

We can safely say that no other genre influenced modern music more than blues. Blues licks, rhythms and harmonies can be found in every music style from rock and heavy metal, to pop and jazz.

A short history and the origins of blues music

Blues first emerged in the mid-19th century in the Deep South of the United States of America.

A huge number of people were brought from Africa to America to serve as slaves for the American citizens. Initially, the African folks were so far-removed from the ideological and cultural background of America that they did not see themselves as playing any part in everyday life. They saw themselves as people that were just brought there to be overworked and used to the point of lethal outcomes. Worse yet, the cruel conditions of those times mandated that the Americans themselves did not see African people as humans at all.

An important sociological and psychological shift happened once the African man started noting and desiring to remedy problems that he saw in the American society. That exact moment is when the shift from African to African American happened. That shift proved to be the fuel for the blues movement. The anger and despair expressed in the songs of the early blues artists was their way of voicing concern and discontent with an American society and culture in which they felt trapped.

Musically speaking, blues was a conglomerate of very different and almost opposite musical influences. On the one hand, you had the African musical heritage that was just part of their DNA. On the other hand, as the slaves spent more and more time in the "land of opportunity," they started to develop some new musical forms as a way of alleviating stress. For example, you had field hollers which were a completely vocal type of expression which used singing to accompany the work that they were doing as well as to vent their feelings of tiredness, fatigue and injustice. The crucial part of the field hollers was the call-and-response pattern that became omnipresent in a variety of contemporary musical styles. Namely, one worker would sing a line in which he expressed his discontent, and then the rest of his peers would echo the line he sang. Other American-created musical forms that came into the melting pot known as blues are chants, shouts and work songs.

One of the blues elements that was derived from other forms of music is the walking bassline. Mostly adapted from jazz greats, also of African American heritage, the walking bassline served as the precursor to what we know as rock 'n' roll riffs of the 1950s and onward.

Subgenres of Blues

Delta blues

Delta blues is one of the earliest styles of blues.

This pioneering blues subgenre got its name from the Mississippi delta, home for many of the blues originators.

If you take into account how old this blues form is, and the dreadful circumstances in which these blues players lived, you can picture the sound of their music.

The Delta blues style is centered around one person: a passionate guitar player who sings about his troubling everyday life in a raw and passionate way.

The highly innovative guitar style was the backbone of this blues style, with many of the Delta blues performers pioneering certain techniques, styles of harmony and songwriting patterns.

Delta blues is blues in its rawest form, straight from the heart. One man, pouring his soul out with no studio gimmickry.

Playing live, he would be accompanied by the minimal line up of bass and very light/ subtle drums.

Notable artists:

- **John Lee Hooker** - One of the best-known exponents of the Delta blues guitar-playing style. Later, he went on to participate in the Detroit blues subgenre.

- **Howlin' Wolf** - This Chicago-born blues guitarist, singer and harmonica player was also highly influential in creating the style of Delta blues.

- **Robert Johnson** - One of the pioneers of the singer-songwriter format and widely recognized as the greatest artist of the Delta blues movement.

He also had an important influence on the early rock 'n' roll musicians.

- **Muddy Waters** - The dictionary definition of a slide guitar giant. Began his career as a Delta blues performer, but reached his peak level of fame within the Chicago blues subgenre.

Chicago blues

The sweet sounds of the Chicago blues music scene have their roots firmly planted in the Delta blues subgenre.

As history would have it, poverty-stricken African Americans in the South were migrating north in large numbers to find work. As they finally started bearing fruit from their work, they were able to afford themselves some electric instruments and the much-needed amplification.

As a result of them being much more equipped, they started to play in bands. The solo performance which was the main hallmark of the Delta blues genre was replaced by the grandiose sound of bands that consisted of guitar players, pianists and bassists.

The louder sound, which was the result of amplification, resulted in those artists being able to play to larger audiences in the Chicago blues clubs.

To the untrained ear, the sound of the Chicago blues would definitely be what first springs to mind when the word "blues" is mentioned.

Notable artists:

- **Willie Clayton** - The epitome of a Chicago blues singer-songwriter, Willie Clayton went on to achieve huge mainstream success, with ten of his albums ending up on the Billboard top charts.

- **Bo Diddley** - One of the pioneers of electric guitar in the blues genre and a hugely influential figure in the realms of blues, rock and roll, and rhythm and blues.

- **Willie Dixon** - What Dr. Dre is to rap, Willie Dixon is to blues. The guy was a double bassist, singer, songwriter and a record producer that helped kickstart the careers of names like Bo Diddley and Muddy Waters. One of the key figures of the Chicago blues movement.

- **Buddy Guy** - Probably the biggest name of the Chicago blues scene in terms of sales and fame. He is an incredibly influential singer, guitar player and songwriter.

- **Sonny Boy Williamson** - This is another huge name in Chicago blues circles. Though not a guitar player, his songwriting and harmonica playing were enormously influential in the whole genre of blues.

Jump blues

The jump blues subgenre was incepted at the tail end of the Big Band era.

It was the late 1940s/early 1950s, and the economic hardships forced many Big Bands to downsize their line-ups into smaller combos.

Once the dance-oriented Big Band sound adopted basic 12-bar blues structure, everything changed.

The sound became more fun, upbeat and straightforward.

The jump blues subgenre was the direct precursor to what we know today as rock 'n' roll.

Notable artists:

- **Louis Jordan** - He was an enormously influential saxophone player and songwriter whose humoristic approach to his licks became a true blueprint for the blues and rock 'n' roll players that were to follow.

- **T-Bone Walker** - One of the best guitar players of all time, and one of the innovators of the jump blues style.

- **Big Joe Turner** - The legendary blues shouter. You may find yourselves asking, "What is a shouter?" Well, it's a person who could sing over the amplified band with no microphone. He was the forefather of rock 'n' roll singing as we know it today. Rest assured, John Lennon wouldn't have sung "Twist and Shout" the way he did if it wasn't for Big Joe Turner.

- **Wynonie Harris** - Another blues shouter with a real feel for the hit. He had fifteen Top Ten hits between 1946 and 1952. In many influential circles, he is also regarded as one of the founding fathers of rock 'n' roll.

Electric blues/Blues rock

The blues undoubtedly gave birth to the legendary sounds of rock 'n' roll.

The crucial role, in that regard, was played by the subgenre of blues called jump blues. As jump blues stripped away all the grandiose instrumentation and focused on the small, but effective, combos playing the 12-bar blues patterns, the blueprint for what was to become rock 'n' roll emerged.

The early rockers took it up a notch in terms of speed, and they also played it with electric instruments at a much higher volume.

Now, imagine the loud instrumentation and the sounds of the electric instruments, but instead of playing faster rock-'n'-roll-type stuff, they are playing something more akin to the Chicago blues style.

And there you have it! The genre of blues rock!

It was within the confines of the blues rock genre that the first white people started to adapt the style of blues with their own musical expression.

Notable artists:

- **Jimi Hendrix** - Widely regarded as the most important instrumentalist of the 20th century.

- **Eric Clapton** - The legendary blues rock guitarist, and the only three-time Rock and Roll Hall of Fame inductee

- **Stevie Ray Vaughan** - One of the biggest mainstream media darlings of the blues genre. Arguably, one of the last guitar heroes.

- **Gary Moore** - Hailing from Northern Ireland, he was one of the main flag wavers for the genre of blues during the 80s and 90s, when certain other genres were taking the spotlight.

- **Joe Bonamassa** - Arguably the most popular contemporary blues guitarist.

Why is it important to know blues to understand modern music?

Whether it's clear to the untrained ear or not, the blues is the foundation of almost all of the modern popular music styles.

It's not just the 12-bar form that makes blues what it is. The instrumentation, the songwriting patterns, the harmony structure: it all found its way to influence various other contemporary styles of music such as jazz, rock, country, soul, R&B, funk and even ska. All of those genres either descended from, developed out of, or were at least influenced by the blues.

You can take any of your other favorite music genres and test our claim.

If you like heavy metal, you know that the pioneering band of heavy metal, Black Sabbath, was first a blues band. The (in)famous tritonus, or the diminished fifth that made the riff of the song, "Black Sabbath," the first ever metal song, is the dark sound of that note, which is also called the blue note.

There is also a noticeable deficiency in the players of younger generations that have skipped the mandatory training in the blues. Although, maybe hard to describe, that deficiency is the direct consequence of not learning to phrase the solos tastefully. As a result, their lead playing tends to sound like a bunch of scales playing one after another.

Since the essence of the blues is the expression of emotion, learning to improvise over those simple chord progressions is the fundamental skill that will serve you in whatever genre you are playing.

The best example is Mr. David Gilmour. The guy managed to paint some of the finest textural soundscapes with very few notes, but with an incredible feel that he got from his blues guitar heroes.

Therefore, the knowledge of blues is the very glue that holds together all of the different technical and theoretical aspects that a person can get into.

Last but not least, since blues is so crucial, yet relatively simple to get into, it is the mandatory language that all players learn. Therefore, it is important to know how to play it so you can jam with other musicians. It is the common place and the first thing that a lot of the bands and groups of musicians tend to start playing. It is very common, everybody knows it, and it makes for a great tool to gel with the other musicians you are playing with.

LEVEL 1

Basic Chords and Form

Like all self-respecting noobs, we need to start right from the beginning with this whole chord thing.

There is definitely no better way to start your basic blues chord journey than with — in all their shimmering majesty — the Seventh Chords!

We'll assume that you are not even familiar with the term open chords, so we'll explain it here just in case. What makes an open chord is quite self-explanatory: the ringing of the open strings. The basic open chords are the ones you usually find within the first three frets on your guitar.

We are going to cover all of their bluesy brothers 'n sisters and one extra chord, just 'cause we're in a good mood today.

P.S. Don't get hung up on the chord names, we'll explain them later. All that theoretical stuff will be dissected in the pages to come, but for now, just pick up your guitar and enjoy!

1.1. Basic chords to play the blues

E7

In order to play this one, just fret your traditional E major chord and instead of fretting the E on the second fret of the fourth string, just let the open string ring out.

It is that simple!

Now, we're gonna take the same basic chord and spice it up just a tad bit!

E7 open chord

In order to play this next one, you fret your regular E7 chord and then add a pinky on the third fret of the second string, as seen below.

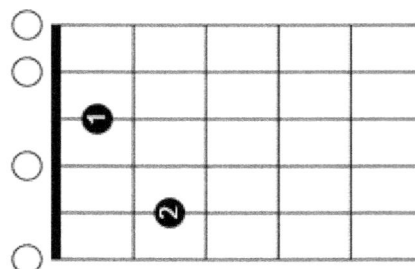

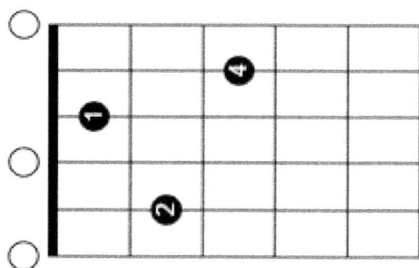

E7 open chord (variant)

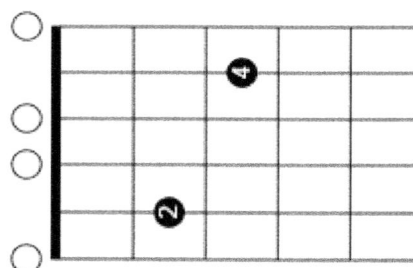

Em7 open chord (variant)

A7

For this A7 chord, you will need to fret the regular A major chord and then remove the finger from the third string, letting it ring out openly.

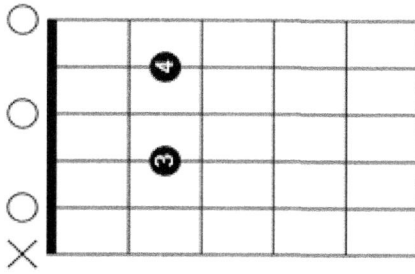

A7 open chord

Let us show you another way of playing the A7 chord in the open position so you can make your blues chord progressions even more sassy!

Fret the A major chord like you'd do normally and then add a finger on the 3rd fret of the 1st string.

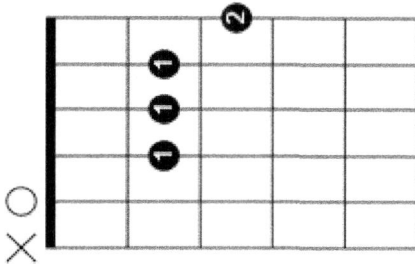

A7 open chord (variant)

D7

The only difference between the D7 chord and the regular D major chord is the fact that the finger is placed on the 1st fret of the 2nd string, instead of the 3rd fret.

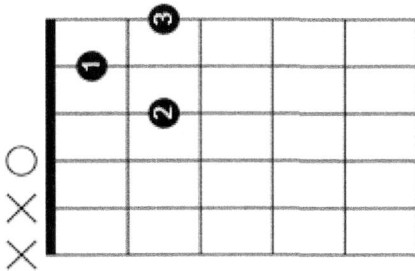

D7 open chord

C7

For now, we're gonna be a bit ageist and leave out the minors here. So, only major chords in regards to C. The minor chords are reserved for later.

Best for last, right?

Anyhow, to play this bad boy, you will need to fret your traditional C major chord and then just add your pinky on the 3rd fret of the 3rd string.

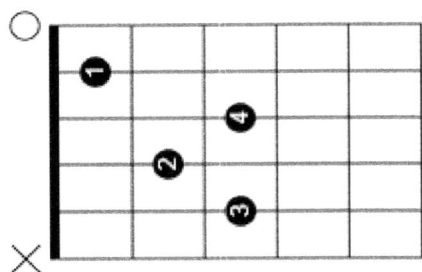

C7 open chord

G7

This one is a tad bit trickier than the ones that came before. You fret the 3rd fret of the 6th string with your ring finger and the 1st fret of the 1st string with your index finger. All the rest of the strings should ring out open, except the 5th string that should be muted with your ring finger.

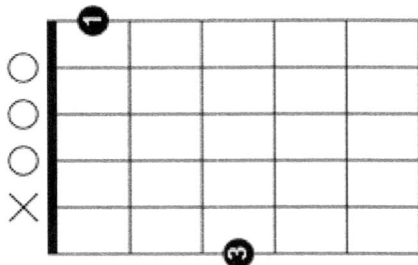

G7 open chord

B7

Same as the previous two, the B7 chord is not worthy of the noob master race.

Since this one is quite different from the natural major chord, you should learn this shape from scratch.

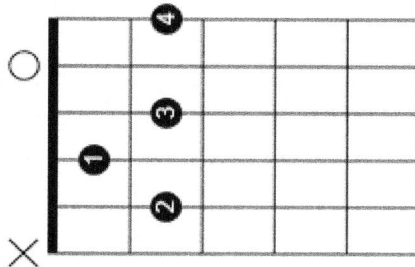

B7 open chord

1.2. Theory 101: Dominant 7th chords

No worries, we are not gonna go batshit crazy with theory here. We're just going to give you enough information so you have the basic understanding of what you're doing for now. That is of the utmost importance for developing the solid basis for the advanced theory concepts, as well as for the mandatory blues jamming with your broskis.

If you know nothing about the way chords are structured, stick with us. If you know your basics, feel free to skip ahead.

One of the main constituent elements of blues are the dominant 7th chords. What gives them their charm is the "unresolved tension" which just flows out of their sonic pores.

Although their full name is dominant 7th chords, that is not the way they appear on music sheets, and rarely even in real-life situations.

If you take a chord that is in the key of A, the way it would be jotted down is A7 .

So, to be clear:

- A major chord – A

- A major chord with a dominant 7th – A7

> **Note:** *Have in mind, if you see a chord that's marked as Amaj7, that's not the same as A7.*

In order to explain the dominant 7th chords, we're going to use one scale — C major.

CDEFGABC

I II III IV V VI VII I

C major scale

Have in mind:

- The letters point to the note of the scale

- The Roman numerals below determine the scale degree of each note within the C major scale.

The C major chord is built upon a C major triad.

The triad consists of the 1st, 3rd and 5th scale degree.

Let's see that within your standard C open chord.

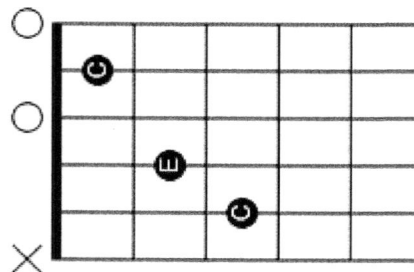

C open chord

Being that your open 3rd and open 1st strings are notes G and E respectively, we can see that a C major chord is only composed of the notes C, E and G.

Although C and E are played twice, they are the same notes, only in different octaves.

If you look at the C major scale degrees, you will see that the notes C, E and G are the 1st, 3rd and 5th scale degrees. That is the blueprint for building major chords in general.

Now that we know what the major chords are, let's move on and understand the Dominant 7th chords.

Once again, we will be in the key of C.

The C7 chord is composed of your standard C major triad with an b7th note from the scale.

Therefore, the chord formula would be:

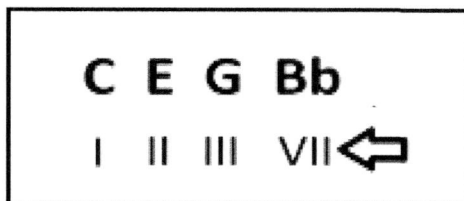

C E G Bb
I II III VII ⬅

The seventh degree of the C minor scale.

C7 chord formula

So, it is by adding the flat 7th note that the dominant 7 chords create that unique sound — an unresolved sound.

   Now let's take a look at the C7 chord again so we can see the chord formula in action:

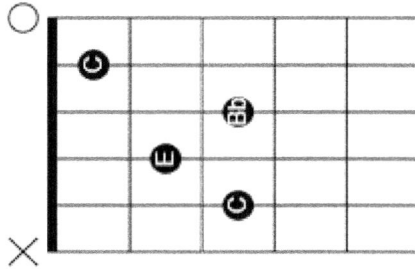

C7 chord chart

1.3. Dominant 9th chords

Theory 101: Dominant 9th chords

For any noob worth his salt, the name of this chord probably sounds scary. As if the 7th wasn't enough already...

But, don't worry. Dominant 9th chord is to dominant 7th chord as cheeseburger is to double cheeseburger — it's only an upgrade.

We'll keep it simple.

The good news is, for the dominant 9th chord to be created, you only need to add one note to the dominant 7th chord.

So, we're almost there...

Let's take another look at our dominant 9th chord formula. This time, we're gonna make it an F9 chord.

F A C Eb G

- the scale degrees are respectively 1, 3, 5, b7, 9

So, you may wonder, "What the heck is a 9th note, when the diatonic scale has only 8 notes?"

If that's the case, you are starting to ask the right questions!

Lucky you, you have us to guide you.

Well, let's take a look at the two octaves of F major scale next to each other:

			I	II	III	IV	V	VI	VII	I
F	G	A	Bb	C	D	E	F	G	A	Bb	C	D	E	F
I	II	III	IV	V	VI	VII	VII	VIII	IX	X	XI	XIII	XIV	XV

F major scale, 2 octaves

So, we clearly see that the 9th note is actually the same as the 2nd note, just an octave higher.

1.4. I – IV – V chords in the key of E

OK, so, to round up this noob chord lesson, we need to show you the elementary blues chord progression.

What is a chord progression?

Well, as the name rather suggests, it is a series of chords in a certain key.

For this chord progression, we are going to be in the key of E. ,

The chords that are featured in this progression are the I, IV and V chords. What does that mean?

Let us show you on the I chord example. The first note (or scale degree) in E major is E, right?

So, the I chord is E7:

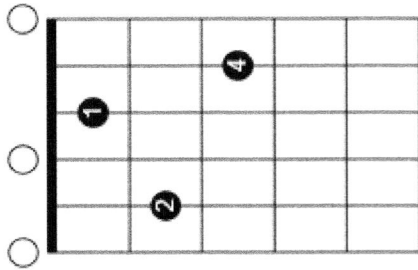

E7 open chord

The fourth note in an E major scale is A, so the IV chord is A7:

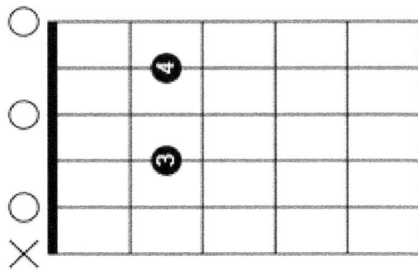

A7 open chord

The fifth note in an E major scale is B, therefore the V chord is B7:

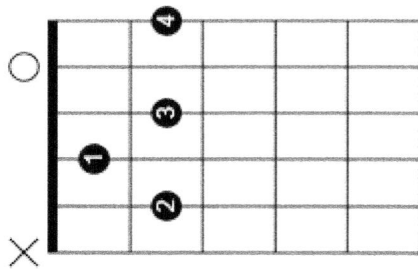

B7 open chord

There you have it! The mother of all blues chord progressions!
We'll get on the topic of chords and chord progressions again, but let's go on to other topics for now!

1.5. What is a Blues form?

The standard blues form is known as the 12-bar blues.

It is a rhythmic and harmonic template for all blues playing. Whether it was the field hollers, the front porch Delta blues guitar masters or just a rock band jamming some blues-inspired songs, they are all going to be doing it with the same template of chord choice and ratio of chord changes.

Being that it's a 12-bar format, there are 12 measures of that pattern.

Those 12 measures can be divided into 3 phrases, with all of them lasting four bars each.

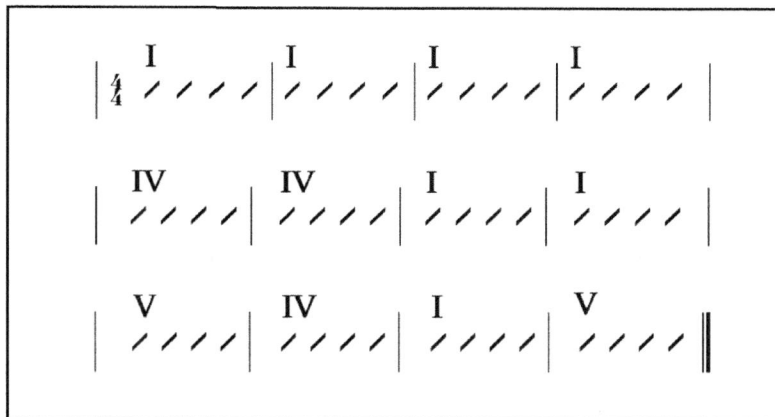

In the pictorial presentation above, you can see all of the 12 measures.

1 measure = 1 chord. The chords are represented in Roman numerals. Each Roman numeral speaks of the scale note upon which the chord was built.

In case of the C major scale, the 12-bar form would look like this:

Blues in C

This 12-bar blues form is designed to be played over and over again. That means that once you reach the C on the 12th measure, you can start all over again from the C on the 1st measure.

1.6. Basic 12-bar blues progression in A

OK, so let's figure out the 12-bar blues progression in the key of A major.

Let's start from the A major scale itself.

If we know the 12-bar blues form, we know that we need the I, IV and V chords.

In the case of the A major scale, those chords would be A, D and E. In order to make it sound more bluesy, we are going to make those chords all dominant 7th chords.

Let's go over those chords in the open position once again.

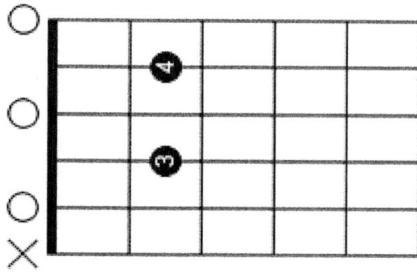

A7

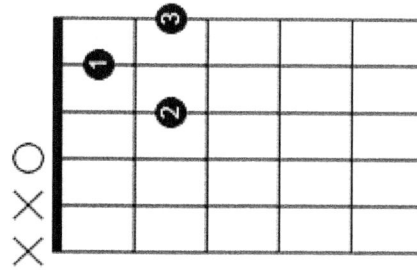

D7

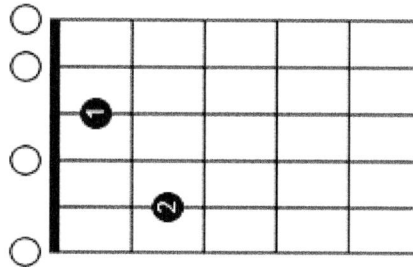

E7

Just in case, let's see the pictorial representation of the 12-bar blues form in the key of A major:

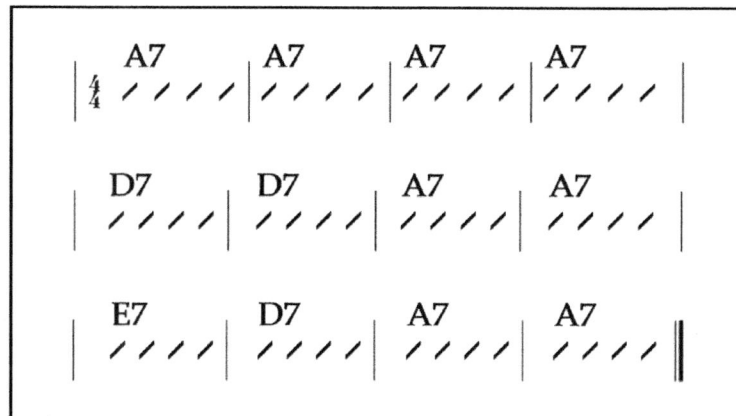

Once again, each chord is worth one measure, or in other words, one bar.

LEVEL 2

Rhythms and Riffs

2.1. What is shuffle?

If there was any justice in the world, dictionaries would include as part of their definition for the listing, America, not only the usual suspects: McDonalds, The Statue of Liberty, etc., but also the subject of today's discussion — the legendary shuffle beat!

All of us, musicians and fans of music alike, know what the shuffle beat is, even if we do not associate said rhythm with its name. That just goes to show how influential and ever-present that beat is.

Even if we don't know the explicit constituent elements of it (we'll get you covered on that one today, no worries), we at least know the way its rhythmic majesty sounds.

The first styles of music that incorporated this type of rhythm were, of course, those stalwarts of modern music: jazz and blues.

It is a known fact that the shuffle beat was indeed the subconscious rhythmic imitation of sounds the trains were making while going down the tracks. Just imagine a scene of a train leaving the Deep South and going to Chicago, let's say.

And there you have it! The sound of the train going down the tracks is what inspired that famous swung 8th note that is the basis of the shuffle rhythm.

Now, not to scare any of you guitar geeks out there, but shuffle is not only reserved for the drummers. You have a lot to offer to that groove as well!

So, let's delve right in!

2.2. Difference between straight and swung 8th note

So, basically, in our standard straight 8th note grooves, we have an even subdivision of the beat into two parts. Both of those two parts can carry two 8th notes, with all of them being at the same distance from each other. So, there's not a lot of explaining we have to do there, since we all know how that sounds.

However, the swung 8th note groove is a somewhat different beast to its aforementioned counterpart. In order to understand it, we need to think in triplets. We get triplets once we evenly subdivide the beat into three parts. Now, in order to make this as painless as possible, take your preferred triplet counting style of choice (whether it's "one-two-three-one-two-three," "one-and-a-two-and-a" or "one-triplet-two-triplet") and leave out the second note, and there you have it! It is that simple!

But, just in case, let's go over it together…If we utilize the "one-two-three-one-two-three" counting, we literally just leave out the "two" every time you count or play.

Now, every "one" beat is the same as it would be in the case of the straight 8th note pattern, but the "three" is an 8th note triplet, which gives it its recognizable swinging feel.

Let's see this simple notation, just to make sure we all got it down right:

Straight 8th notes

Swung 8th notes

Now, let's see how both straight and shuffle beats look when using just the open 6th string:

Straight 8th notes - open 6th string

Swung 8th notes - open 6th string

2.3. How to practice with a metronome?

The best way to develop your sense of rhythm is to practice with a metronome. Practicing with a metronome will make you a much more disciplined player and will instill a great inner sense of timing in your playing.

The philosophy of practicing with a metronome is very simple. The general rule of thumb is to set the metronome at a comfortable tempo for the given phrase you are about to practice.

The tempo is often marked as BPM, which stands for beats per minute. The higher the number of beats per minute, the higher the speed at which you are meant to play.

Again, don't rush things and don't fool yourself that you are able to play something at a higher tempo than you actually can. We have all been there, and we can tell you, practicing things at a higher tempo than what you are comfortable with is a surefire way to gain some habits that will be very hard to get rid of later on.

Instead, you should start practicing at reasonable tempos from the start so you instill the best playing habits possible.

Nowadays, metronomes are available in numerous different forms. You can use them for free on certain websites, there are certain downloadable metronome apps, and then there are also your physical metronomes, which can come in both digital and analog form.

Whatever your metronome of choice may be, it is the mandatory tool for practice.

Now, back to practicing philosophy: Once you are comfortable playing that phrase at a certain speed, you can further increase the tempo. Now, be careful not to increase it way too much. The tempo should be increased incrementally so you develop the true mastery of that concrete phrase that you are practicing.

A great tip is to start practicing a phrase at a comfortable tempo, and then increase it by 10 BPMs. After that becomes comfortable, you decrease the tempo by 5 BPM, and then you start the circle from the top.

That way you are constantly shocking your system just a tad bit, and then going back to perfect the BPM count you have skipped.

Backbeat

Backbeat is the most common type of beat in the world of popular music.

It is common time — 4/4 — and in a typical drumming scenario, the drummer would play a kick drum on the 1st and the 3rd beat of the measure.

Accenting on 2 and 4

The fact that in the backbeat scenario the snare drum hits would go on the 2nd and 4th beat, makes those two the "accented ".

2.4. Basic blues riff in E

Now, the 12-bar blues patterns that we have covered so far are all chord-based progressions.

What we are about to show you is the basic blues riff in the 12-bar blues form.

If you are not sure what a riff is, let us cover that for you.

A riff is a repetitive musical sequence usually played on the lower strings of a guitar.

Here is a basic blues riff in E, loosely based on playing mainly simple power chord shapes.

Note : Audio track available in bonus section

2.5. Basic blues riff in A

Here is another example following the same style of riff in the key of A. Starting from the 5th position.

Now, other than the riffs, blues is also very famous for its walking riffs played on the lower strings.

2.6. Walking bass shuffle riff

So, usually, you would have instruments in the upper registers playing the moving melodies, while the parts in the lower registers would be there to support the steady, fixed bass lines.

Another novelty that blues brought to the forefront is that you could have the parts in the lower registers also playing some tasty riffs with meandering notes.

Let us show you one of the steady bass line examples.

LEVEL 3

Scales Without Fail

3.1. - Major pentatonic and minor pentatonic

These are two of the crucial scales that you need to play the blues.

The main innovation in these scales comes from its pentatonic form. Your traditional western scale is a diatonic scale consisting of 7 notes. The pentatonic scale only consists of 5 notes, which gives a modern sound to it. It already sounds like a melody.

Major pentatonic

Before we jump into major pentatonic, let's look at the major scale first, so we can see how the major pentatonic emerges from the natural major scale.

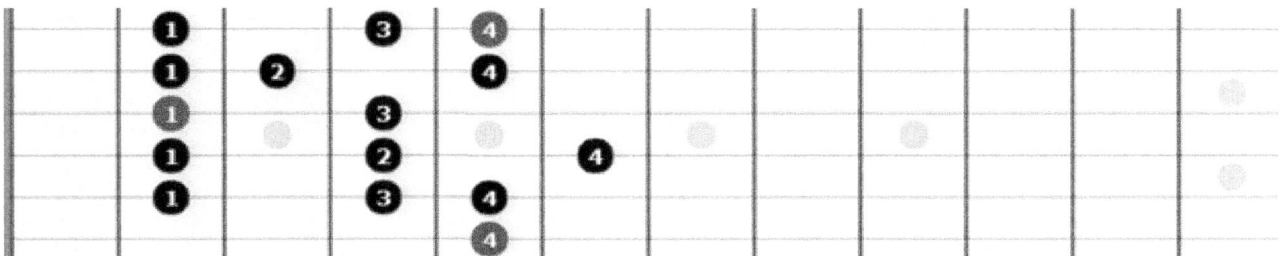

Now, we see from the A major scale that it features 7 different notes. Since pentatonic scale literally means "five-tone scale," we have to figure out which two notes we should expel from the major scale to get the major pentatonic.

First, let's take a look at the major pentatonic scale in the key of A:

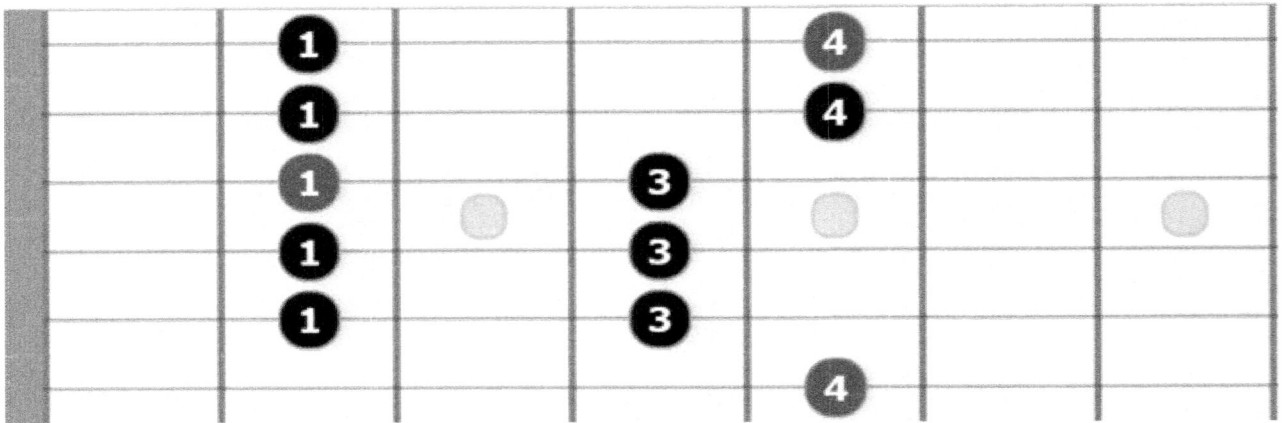

If we compare figure 29 and figure 30, we see that in order to derive the major pentatonic scale from the standard major scale, we need to get rid of the note on the 5th fret of the 5th string and the note on the 6th fret of the 4th string. In terms of scale degrees, it would be the 4th and the 7th scale degree.

You can use this same pattern/ formula to find pentatonic scales in all keys across the fretboard.

> **Tip** : Remove 4th and 7th degree of the major scale to get major pentatonic

Minor pentatonic

Now, in order to get the minor pentatonic scale from the regular minor scale, we should look at the minor scale first.

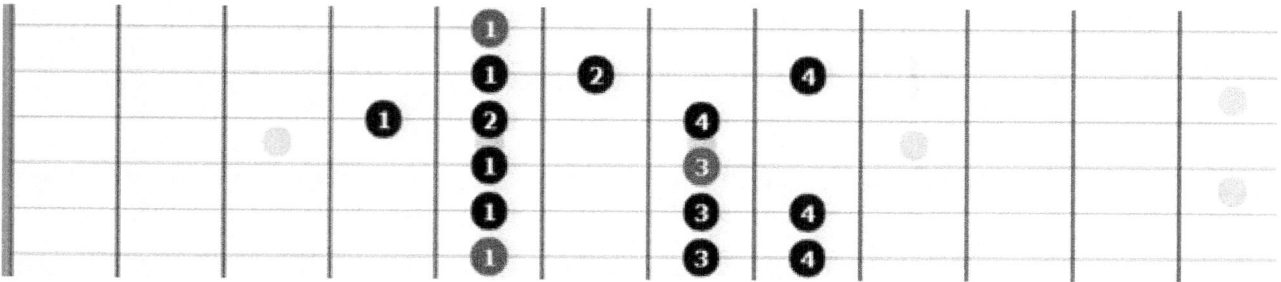

Minor pentatonic scale in the key of A:

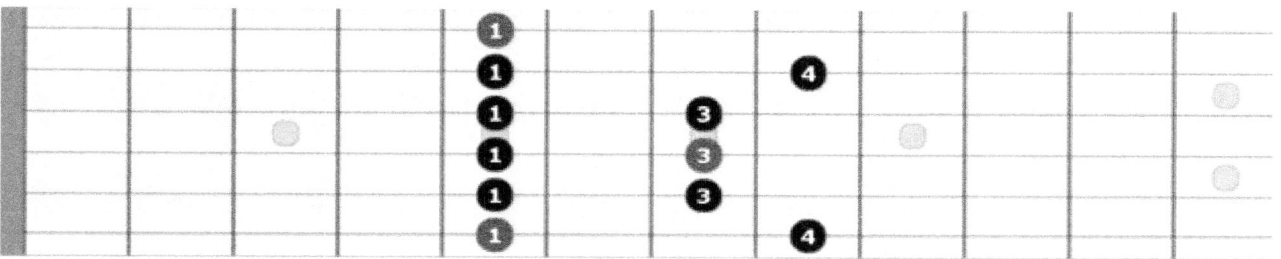

If we compare the minor scale to the minor pentatonic, we see that we need to chuck 2 notes out in order to derive the pentatonic scale. The notes we need to leave out are to be found on the 7th fret of the 6th string and the 8th fret of the 5th string. Also, their respective octaves pictured on this diagram (4th fret of the 3rd string, and the 6th fret of the 2nd string) are to be left out if we are to play the pure pentatonic scale. In terms of scale degrees, they are the 2nd and 6th scale degree. This formula can be used to derive minor pentatonic scales out of regular minor scales in all keys all across the fretboard.

3.2. - What is a Blue note?

The blue note is an integral part of blues and jazz music. It is a note that is sung or played at a slightly different pitch from the standard western scale. That is done for expressive purposes, and the note is usually pitched a quarter tone or a semitone up or down.

The common blue notes: lowered third, lowered fifth and lowered seventh scale degrees. The lowered fifth can be also called a raised fourth.

3.3. - What is a Blues scale?

People tend to think like this: pentatonic scale = blues scale, but that isn't really the case.

The penta in pentatonic scale stands for 5, meaning that the pentatonic scale is a 5-note scale.

In those terms, the blues scale can be considered as a hexatonic scale, since it consists of 6 notes.

Blues scales consist of all the notes of the pentatonic scale, plus a "blue note."

In the case of minor pentatonic blues scale, the added blue note is the lowered fifth (or the raised fourth).

For example, blues scale in the key of A:

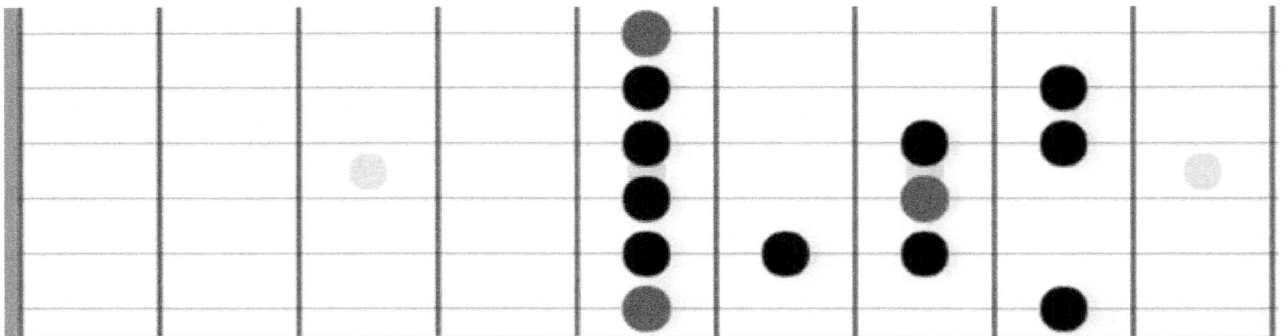

Same note on its relative, the major pentatonic, features the flat third as its blue note.

Therefore, the major pentatonic blues scale in the key of A:

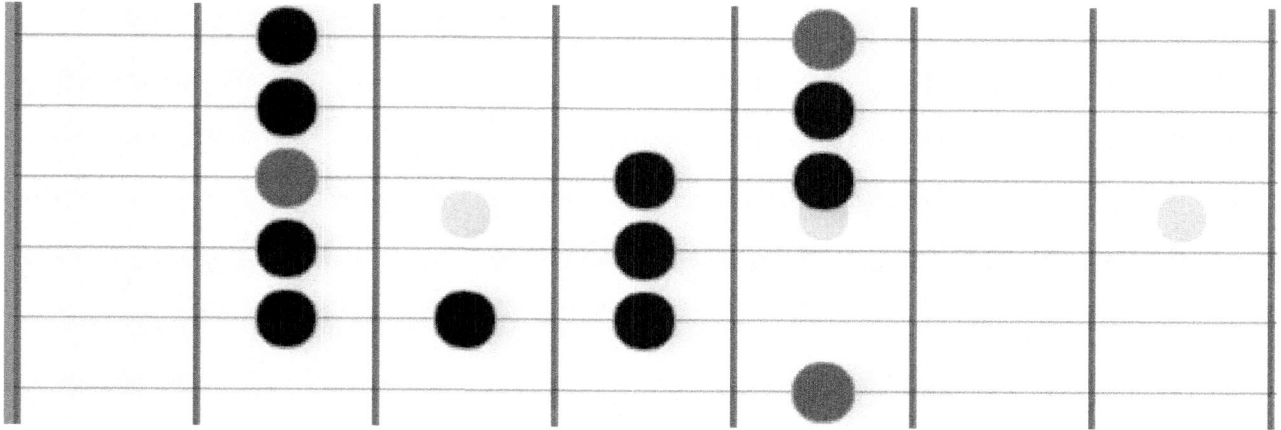

3.4. What scale to play over I chord?

Well, navigating through this chord is really quite easy.

If you are playing over a minor blues chord progression, your I chord will definitely be a minor chord, therefore you should play the minor pentatonic blues scale while that chord is being played underneath.

If you find yourself in a major blues chord progression, that's a bit of a different story.

Quite literally, this is where the magic of blues begins. If the I chord is a dominant chord, you have a couple of options.

Playing a major pentatonic scale over a major chord is quite straightforward. Yes, you can do that.

A mixolydian over A7? Yes, that's a good option too.

Lots of people play minor pentatonic on the dominant chord, but to me, it sounds incomplete because minor pentatonic doesn't have the 3rd of the I chord. So, it doesn't address the tonality of the I chord.

What we have here is an incomplete scale that is unable to address the chord. And that makes it safe to play over I or even over the whole blues progression to some extent.

However, a cool trick would be playing minor pentatonic up a 5th! If your I chord is A7, that means play E minor pentatonic over A7 chord.

3.5. What scale to play over IV chord?

In a minor blues scenario, it is very straightforward.

You play your minor blues pentatonic scale and it will sound great.

However, in a major blues scenario, you can use minor pentatonic or minor blues pentatonic scales.

 If you were playing the major blues pentatonic scale over the one chord, playing the minor blues pentatonic scale over the major IV chord would sound mind-bogglingly cool and exotic.

For example, you can use Am pentatonic or A blues scale over D7 chord, which is the IV chord in A blues.

Don't forget: you could also use D mixolydian over D7 chord as well.

3.6. What scale to play over V chord?

The V chord is the place where you can go really crazy in terms of note selection.

You have quite a few options to play over V chords. You could use the mixolydian scale, the altered scale, mixolydian with b9 and other hip-sounding scales.

But as a beginner, you don't have to start with all of them.

Remember when I said you can use minor pentatonic up a 5th over a dominant chord? You can use the same concept on the V chord too.

On E7, use B minor pentatonic for a start.

One of the coolest tips or tricks to utilize in in the quest for making your V chord licks as tasty as they can be is to use what we call a "BB box."

Don't worry, Guitar Head's not gonna leave you high and dry on the "BB box" thing, we're gonna show it to you in a matter of a couple of pages.

Use the backing tracks that you are getting with this book to play around with this scale and come up with your own unique ways of implementing it over the different chords.

3.7. Mixolydian Mode

For the sake of making as much sense as possible, let's stick to the key of A for explaining this one.

If you are soloing over a dominant chord, the clichéd choice would be mixolydian mode. So, let's learn the scale.

First of all, we've got to make sure you guys know how to play the mixolydian mode.

Without getting into too much theory, the mixolydian mode is very similar to the standard major scale.

Just play your basic major scale, but with a lowered 7th.

Here's the A mixolydian scale in two octaves.

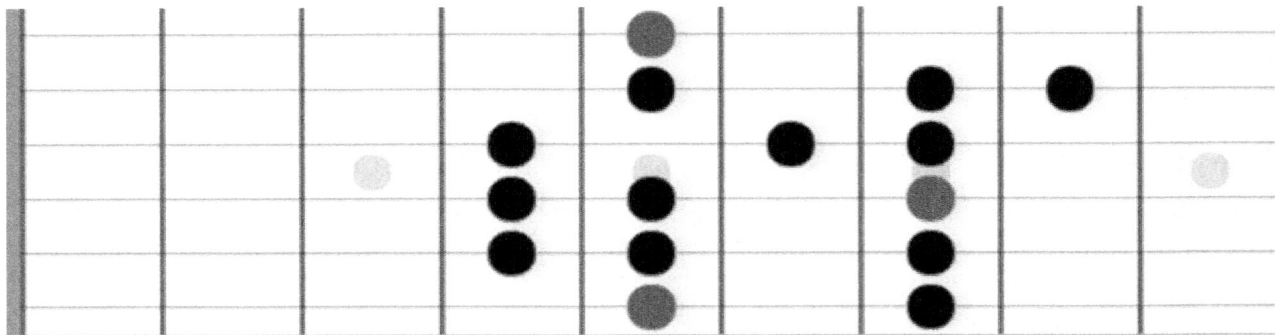

3.8. Soloing over blues progression

Blues is an art form of improvised music. When it comes to improvisation, one can use many tools to express what they feel in the moment. But for a start, we are going to use scales to improvise over the 12-bar blues progression here.

Most noobs try to solely play one minor pentatonic over the blues progression. It succeeds in sounding cutesy, but fails to address the chords and ultimately sounds weak.

Blues soloing is about soloing over changes, that means you need different tactics for each chord. It is advantageous to your creativity to learn how to manipulate all of these different chords in the blues context.

Let me break down what will be your go-to scale to play over I (A7) chord, IV (D7) chord and V (E7) chord in A blues.

3.9. BB Box on I chord

Who is BB king?

Born as Riley B. King in 1925, our beloved B.B. really lived up to his surname.

Nowadays, he is heralded as "The King of Blues" and is among the most influential electric guitar players of all genres.

The contributions he is best known for are his unique string bends, the vibrato oozing with feel and emotion, and staccato picking — the combined result of these techniques has cemented him as one of the most legendary guitar players with some of the most tasteful licks up his sleeve.

DENVER AUGUST 13 BB KING legendary blues guitarist performs in concert August 13, 2002 at Fiddlers Green Amphitheater in Denver, CO. @ TDCPhoto

He was born on a cotton plantation in Mississippi and first fell in love with music while singing in the church choir. During his career that spanned eight decades, he recorded 43 studio albums and played more than 200 shows every year, even into his seventies.

Now, there are not many things in music that go as well together as I chords and B.B. King's plethora of innovations that he brought to the world of music.

There are only a handful of guitar players out there that have as many groundbreaking contributions to the music world as the King himself. Although his technique was highly innovative and his sound often imitated (but never quite matched), his main contributions could easily be the feel that he brought to guitar playing, as well as the famous "BB box."

All of you blues veterans out there are probably yawning at this point, but hey, let's make sure the kids are alright also (hats off to Mr. Townsend, of course, and sorry Mr. Harper!).

What B.B. King did continuously, which influenced all guitar players, even to this day, is play his tasty minor pentatonic blues licks, and then all of a sudden, play some weird major-sounding notes over the I chord. It was the major pentatonic scale with some minced minor notes and some chopped blue notes and chromatic passages. That was a total game changer that made his palette of sonic colors even richer.

Interval formula for BB box

Starting from the root note, the scale has a major 2nd, minor 3rd, perfect 4th, perfect 5th and major 6th

To make things even cooler, he managed to squish all of that harmonic bonanza into a convenient box position in which you could, in a space of four frets, create some of those wonderful sounds that we love and know him for.

So, what we've decided to do today is, we're gonna teach you some of those legendary licks, str8 outta BB box! Oh, wait, that's a completely different genre... Nevermind...Ooops...

Let's just get straight to the point!

Lick no.1

In this wonderful lick, you have the ultimate signature "B.B. trick," which is the major 6th among the minor pentatonic blues notes. In this case, it is the F# note that you play on the 11th fret of the 3rd string. You also have the descending chromatic run which serves as a perfect tool to spice up your melodic dictionary.

Lick no.2

This one goes out to all of you major pentatonic scale purists out there!

Lick No.3

"The best of both worlds," as one bright mind once so brilliantly suggested:

Lick No.4

Sorry Mr. Gallagher, I can't stop crying my heart out (wipes the tears after playing the lick)

Lick No.5

Save the best for last, huh?

These are some of the most influential passages and licks in the history of electric guitar. Not only are they mandatory in prestigious blues and even jazz circles, but they are the groundwork upon which modern-day guitar playing is built!

3.10. Albert King box on IV chord

Who is Albert King?

Albert Nelson, better known by his stage name, Albert King, was one of the most popular and most influential guitar players of all time. Along with B.B. King and Freddie King, the three of them were known as the "Kings of Blues." On a side note, these three are not related, which is a popular misconception.

By Grant Gouldon · https://www.flickr.com/photos/grantdeassmann/20359097662, CC BY-SA 2.0, https://commons.wikimedia.org/w/index.php?curid=9929426

He was a left-handed guitar player that usually played the right-handed guitars turned upside down. He was famous for using different open tunings. Besides that, one of the most interesting idiosyncrasies regarding our man Albert was that he never used the 6th string.

He was one of the first guitar players to popularize the Gibson Flying V shape, and his 1967 album, "Born Under a Bad Sign," is considered to be one of the most essential blues albums.

The Albert King box is probably not as exotic sounding as the BB box, but it can be considered the more fundamental of the two.

Again, let's think within the A minor scale framework:

First of all, you may notice that the Albert King box is somewhat reminiscent of your traditional open D minor chord shape. Well, that is no coincidence.

In contrast with the BB box, this one is more associated with the minor blues playing. You could use this box over IV chord (D7) of A.

On the diagram above, you can see that the root note (A in this case) is colored red.

Besides being the primer of all things minor blues, this one can be an incredibly adventurous tool in the hands of a masterful blues guitar player.

Namely, you can use the somewhat conservative notes from this box and bend them to certain pitches to create some majestic soundscapes.

As far as our root note goes (10th fret of the 2nd string), we can bend it one-and-a-half steps and hit the minor 3rd (C) of A.

If you are feeling lucky, you can try and bend it two whole steps. That way you will get a major third sound, which can spice things up quite nicely if you use it as a passing note. On a side note, you can bend it a whole step and hit a cool 9th sound.

As far as your G note (8th fret of the 2nd string) goes, you can bend it a whole step.

With the C note (8th fret of the 1st string), you can bend it a whole step as well as half a step. Be wary though, with the half-step bend, you are stepping into the major blues territory. If used accordingly, it can be a great addition to your lick arsenal.

With your D note (10th fret of the 1st string), you can use it to bend a whole step as well as the half step. The half-step bend from the D note will get you a flat fifth, AKA our beloved "blue note," which is literally a centerpiece of the minor blues guitar playing.

Lick no.1

Baby steps first, as many bright minds used to point out in the past!

This one is an easy lick that features some tasty bends and is great for soloing over the I chord.

Lick no.2

This one is a great example of all the harmonic avenues you venture into with just these five notes. It is mainly achieved by playing some tasteful bends. This one is a great example of a lick you can play over the IV chord.

Lick no.3

This one is great for practicing vibrato. The spacing between plucking the notes really makes for a good foundation to develop your vibrato technique.

Lick no.4

Now, this is the one to solve all your vibrato problems!

Lick no. 5

With this one, you are reaping all of the benefits of the Albert King box.

If there was an AK box video game, this one would be the "final boss" you need to defeat to finish the game.

All of the notes are here, as well as some exotic bends.

LEVEL 4

Essential Blues Techniques

4.1. Bends

No, we are not about to teach you the necessary techniques to play that classic Radiohead album.

OK millennials, don't run away screaming after we say this, but we are about to show you some serious boomer stuff. After all, without blues, there wouldn't be any of the hip modern music styles that we know today, right?

Right.

Essentially, the bends, or the technique of "bending," equates to increasing the pitch of the note with our fretting hand.

Traditionally, we achieve that effect by bending our strings toward the ceiling, except for the top two strings (5th and 6th), which we pull in the direction of the floor.

Whole Tone Bend

All of you seasoned veterans (if there are any of you reading this) can skip the next paragraph.

This one goes out to all of our newbie homeboys out there!

We all know now what bends are, right?

Well, now we need to understand different degrees to which we bend our strings.

Whole-step intervals can be found on the 2nd fret away from the note you are playing. For example, a whole step above the note on the 3rd fret of the 1st string can be found on the 5th fret of the same string.

The goal with the whole-step bends is to increase the pitch of the fretted note so it turns into the note of the second fret up the fretboard on the same string.

If we are fretting the 15th fret of the 2nd string, and we want to bend that note for a whole step, we should pull the string toward the ceiling in order to achieve the pitch of the note that is usually found on the 17th fret of the same string.

One of the things that you need to take into account when practicing bends is the tonal precision of the note you are getting. The easiest way to do that is to play the note that is two frets higher up the fretboard on the same string and then try to match its pitch with the note you are bending.

That way you are guaranteed to install some very healthy bending habits into your guitar playing.

And trust us, you don't want to have to correct the bad habits you have already formed. It's literally hell.

So, listen to our advice and make sure you are practicing bends in this way we have suggested.

Semi- Tone Bend

It is the same movement, the same technique, as the whole-tone bend, it's just that our target note is halfway closer to our original fretted note.

For example, if we are fretting the 11th fret of the 1st string with our bend, we want to achieve the tonality of the 12th fret of the same string by increasing the pitch of the fretted note for just a half step.

And, voila! There you have it, the semitone bend in all its glory!

Again, one of the things that you need to take into account when practicing bends is the tonal precision of the note you are getting.

The easiest way to do that is to play the note that is one fret higher up the fretboard on the same string and then try to match its pitch with the note you are bending.

4.2. Where can you do the whole- step bends within the minor pentatonic box?

For the sake of explaining this, let's imagine we are playing an A minor pentatonic in a couple of positions.

On the diagram below, the notes you can bend for a whole step are marked in circles.

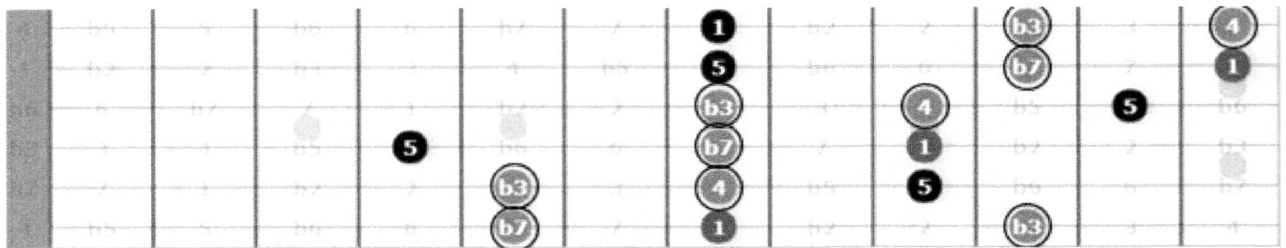

The numbers and the accidentals that you can see in these circle shapes are the scale degrees. Since this is a movable shape, you can implement the same template on all of the other minor pentatonic boxes.

For example, if we move this whole pattern a whole step down, so we have a G minor pentatonic scale, we should still do the whole-step bends on the same scale degrees of flat 7th, flat 3rd, and 4th.

4.3. Vibrato

Along with bending and other cool techniques we are about to show you here, the vibrato is one of the most expressive things you can do on your guitar.

After all, instrumentation started out imitating the human voice, and there are very few (if any) qualities that are as vocal as the vibrato itself.

Now, what is a vibrato you may wonder…

Well, it is a series of bends and returns to the original fretted pitch.

You can do it with the whole-step bends, semi-tone bends; you can do it fast, and slow...Whatever turns your crank, man!

Slow vibrato

One of the parameters of your vibrato is definitely the speed at which you oscillate your bends.

You can do it really slowly, at approximately every quarter note of a beat.

The speed at which you change the pitch of the note does not have to affect the width of your vibrato. Meaning, you can still play a wide whole-step vibrato at a slower speed.

> **Note** : Audio track available in bonus section

Fast, aggressive vibrato

You can spice up your playing and add some much-needed intensity at certain points by playing a fast, aggressive type of vibrato.

You can make it approximately as fast as 16th note triplets.

The aggressive vibrato can be played with both wide and single-step bend depths.

4.4. Rakes

Now, this is like the fine wine of blues guitar playing tricks.

It really is a truly amazing way of making your solos much more expressive and potent.

The technique implements a series of muted adjacent strings before playing a fully ringing note.

Now, some of you may wonder, is it like sweep picking but with muted lower notes?

Well, it does feature a sweeping motion. However, the muted notes we are hitting with our right hand do not have to be played in a specific pitch, time or rhythmic pattern. You just need to land successfully on the desired note you actually want to play.

4.5. Simple slide with fingers

Now, just so you don't get confused, we are not talking about performing this technique with that cool bottle-like thing that they call a slide. We are (for now) focusing on the fine art of sliding with your fingers.

Now, you may think, what the hell is a finger slide then? Well, it's a pretty cool technique that features you picking one note and then playing the next one without any picking. With the finger slide, you are using the same finger to play that next note. Meaning, you are sliding with your finger from the first note on to the next.

Sliding minor 3rd to major 3rd

If there is just one thing to take from this book, it might be this super cool trick. It is one of the most used (and for a good reason!) blues tricks ever.

What you do is slide from your minor 3rd just one fret up to your major 3rd. Let's take, for example, the key of D minor. In that case, you would be playing F as your minor 3rd. If you just slide one fret up to the note F#, you would get your much-needed major 3rd.

Approaching your chord from half step above, or half step below

The same principle you would use to achieve the effect of sliding from minor to major 3rd can be used with chords.

Play any of the chords you have learned just one fret up and slide the chord to where it's supposed to be on the fretboard.

What makes it even cooler is the fact that you can fret the chord one fret up and then slide back one fret to where that chord is intended to be played. Cool, cool stuff.

4.6. Double stops

Yeah, the name of this technique might seem somewhat mysterious and certainly more complicated than the actual concept really is. It's literally nothing more than fretting and picking two notes at the same time.

Playing double stops using 6ths and 3rds

You can, of course, play double stops using all other intervals (just type in Mateus Asato on YouTube, for crying out loud), but for blues licks, you are generally going to play 6ths and 3rds in the double stop form.

Theory 101 Genie: Intervals: 6ths and 3rds

In order to understand the theory behind these intervals, we need to think outside our traditional blues 5 note (pentatonic) scale. For this example, let's think about the traditional C major scale.

The C major scale consists of 7 notes, and to find the 6th interval of every note in the scale, you can just pick any note you like and find the note that is the 6th degree away from the note you have picked.

Let's find the 6th of the note C in the C major scale:

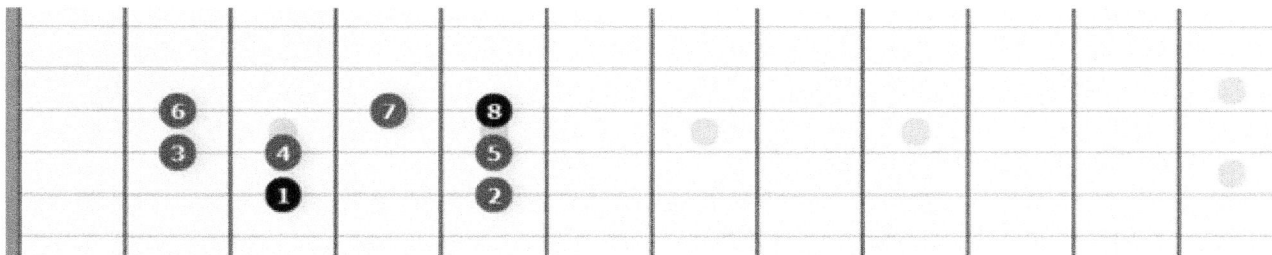

In the C major scale scenario, the C note is the root note, hence it is marked as no.1 and no.8 in this scale diagram.

If we count six scale degrees up from the note C (no.1), we will stop at no.6, which is the note A.

That's how you get your 6th interval, whether the major or minor scales are in question.

Now, let's see how this applies to finding the 3rd interval.

It is exactly the same. You pick the desired scale degree and count up three scale degrees — there is your 3rd interval.

To illustrate this, we will be using the C minor scale.

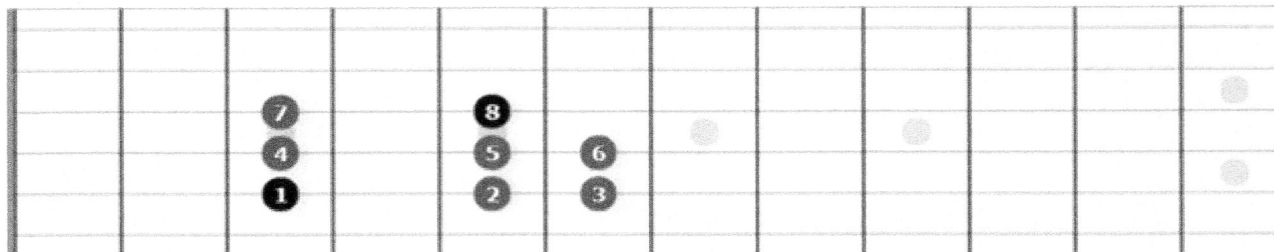

Let's take the second degree of this scale. In the case of C minor, it is the note D. If we count three scale degrees up, we stumble upon note no.4, which is the note F. If we play the C note and the F note at the same time, we get an interval we call the 3rd.

3 blues licks using 6ths and 3rds

Lick no.1

This is a lick that every guitar player should know, no matter what genre they play.

Lick no.2

This one is like the definition of tasty. Another crucial lick for any self-respecting guitar player out there.

Lick no.3

Now, that's a thing of beauty! Right?

4.7. 10 blues licks

Licks in the style of blues greats

Lick no.1

This one is the epitome of B.B. King's playing style. You can see the minor/major third twist in this lick, as well as those tasty bends which enrich the tonal capabilities of the pentatonic scale.

Lick no.2

This C# minor pentatonic lick is the epitome of Albert King's playing style. You can see the typical Albert King box in the works with this tasty lick.

Lick no.3

This A minor pentatonic lick, in the style of Eric Clapton, is one of the most popular licks in all guitar music.

Lick no.4

This is a lick in the style of Stevie Ray Vaughan. One of the main hallmarks of his bluesy licks is the usage of the 9th interval, which can be seen in this lick.

Let's take a look at some other licks that are a bit longer than the ones we have shown you thus far.

4 bar licks over I chord

Lick no.1

Here's an example of a hybrid pentatonic blues lick in A.

Lick no.2

Here's a cool 4 bar major pentatonic lick in A.

2 bar licks over IV chord

Lick no.1

A minor pentatonic lick.

Lick no.2

A major pentatonic lick.

Licks on V chord

Lick no.1

Lick no.2

LEVEL 5

Turn Around

5.1. What is a turnaround?

Although there are turnarounds in different styles of music, we will be focusing on the blues variant of this cool template. The blues turnaround is a musical figure that is played over the last two bars of the 12-bar blues — over the chords I and V. The main function of the turnaround is to set up the tension that resolves by leading into the next repetition of the chord progression.

5.2. Simple turnaround: Approaching the V chord from a half step up

There are not many things that are as simple, yet effective as this.

5.3. Root pedal type turnaround

Now, what would a root-pedal-type turnaround be? Well, it means that the root1 note is droning while we are playing the lick.

In this example, we will be in the key of E:

The lick we're about to show you is straight outta the hands of the OG blues master — Robert Johnson

Let's take a look at the same RJ lick in the key of A:

5.4. Pentatonic scale-based turn around

Here's an incredible pentatonic-based turnaround lick in E minor. This is the lick you would likely hear blues greats such as Eric Clapton and Stevie Ray Vaughan play:

♩ = 110

E⁷

The identical lick in the key of B minor:

♩ = 110

B⁷

5.5. 1-6-2-5 Jazz blues turnaround in Bb

♩ = 110

Bb⁷   Gm⁷   Cm⁷   Dm⁷/F   Bb⁷   F⁷

5.6. 10 different turnarounds

Here are ten more turnarounds in different keys. Use them wisely, fellas!

Turnaround in A no.1

Turnaround in A no.2

Turnaround in E no.1

Turnaround in E no.2

Turnaround in G no.1

Turnaround in G no.2

Turnaround in B no.1

Turnaround in B no.2

Turnaround in Bb no.1

Turnaround in Bb no.2

LEVEL 6

Phrasing and Improvisation

6.1. What is phrasing?

The best way to get the gist of this idea is to compare musical phrasing to lingual phrasing. If we look at individual notes as words, the equivalent of the whole sentence would be the musical phrase. In other words, phrases are a series of notes and making them lyrical is an art form. If you just play the scale up and down, it is as if you are just listing words with no meaning tying them together. Playing tasteful phrases means playing an emotionally packed series of notes, often embellished with tasty vibrato and bends. Now, have in mind, as with writing words, the sentences can be long and short, they can end with question marks as well as one or three dots. All of those emotional states can be portrayed with your playing, and that's exactly where the phrasing comes in. There are not that many genres that rely as heavily upon tasteful phrasing as the blues does. That's why it is the genre that is your best bet to begin your phrasing journey.

6.2. How to create a singable melody? How to give rest? What to play/what not to play?

If we rewind quite a bit to the earliest days of humans developing instruments, we will most certainly find that all of the instruments were created to mimic the human voice. Guitar is no expectation. Perhaps the art of blues soloing is the style in which that vocal attribute of the guitar came into full force. Making the guitar "cry" and using it to express the deepest innermost feelings of oppression was one of the main coping ingredients utilized by the enslaved African American community.

In order to create singable melodies, you must understand that you are not trying to continuously run the scales up and down the neck. Non-linear playing is one of the main hallmarks of lyrical melodies. Giving rest between the phrases is literally like the vocal line taking a break between the verses. It is a hugely important part of the blues style, as it creates spaces and builds tension between the phrases.

6.3. Basics of Call and Response

Call and Response is one of the most fundamental components of the blues — self-explanatory too. A must-know trick for improvisation, and an easy concept to understand, if you feel it in your heart.

I can only explain this with music, not with words!

Let's take Muddy Water's, "Hoochie Coochie Man," a classic example of how call and response happens between vocal phrase and instrumental phrase.

The song starts with the lyric, "Gypsy women told my mother." Consider this a musical question. Immediately in the next phrase, this question is answered by a short instrumental hook. This pattern follows throughout the song and creates an interesting conversation between Muddy Water's voice and the band.

Why do those lyrical-instrumental exchanges qualify as call and response? Set the book aside and listen to the song right now. You'll get what I mean.

Another example would be B.B. King's, "Three O'Clock Blues." Just type the song title on YouTube and listen to the trio live performance of it. Each vocal phrase is answered with a guitar solo. It seems like a man conversing with his guitar.

This tradition/technique pervades the entire blues genre, and it is not only reserved for the guitar/voice combo. It evolved from the response being the mere repetition of the preceding line, to a variation on a given theme, and both can be heard in almost all blues songs of all eras.

Here are five classic call and response examples for you to check out:

6.4. Five examples of Call and Response

1. Robert Johnson - Crossroads

Around the 0:14 mark of this legendary piece you can hear one of the classic examples of call and response.

2. BB King - Lucille

Around the 0:54 mark of this legendary piece you can hear one of the classic examples of call and response.

3. Albert King - Born Under A Bad Sign

Around the 0:17 mark of this legendary piece you can hear one of the classic examples of call and response.

4. Stevie Ray Vaughan - Texas Flood

Around the 1:10 mark of this legendary piece you can hear one of the classic examples of call and response.

5. Joe Bonamassa - Stop!

Around the 0:32 mark of this legendary piece you can hear one of the classic examples of call and response.OK. But how do I learn it?

Here are five call and response examples for you to practice. For each lick, you play a 2-bar phrase as call, and then "respond" with another 2-bar phrase. I would suggest listening to the audio track first — you will better absorb the chemistry between the two different phrases. You can see I have marked those two phrases as "Call" and "Response" above the TAB.

You can learn all of them as they are and then experiment with them. Probably, you can come up with different responses for these existing calls.

Lick 1

Lick 2

Lick 3

Lick 4

Lick 5

Learn and internalize the call and response concept before you start playing with our resident guitarist in Level 8. Yes, we have a whole chapter dedicated for you to practice call and response

LEVEL 7

2 Blues Solos with Transcription

So far, we've learned most of the essential things a blues guitarist must know. We've discussed form, chord progressions, scales, licks, tricks and more. This will help build your vocabulary to play blues. But the next question is: How can one incorporate all these into their playing — let's say, during improvisation or composing? We've seen what to play over I chord and what to play over V chord, but how can we mix these two separate ideas to fit into the progression? How to intertwine these ideas and make it sound like they're flowing into each other, rather than existing as isolated "copy and paste" licks?

Well, my friend, the answer is simple! Just listen to blues solos played by the maestros. Spend ample amount of time listening to solos; get it under your finger; try learning it the way it is. Analyze it, listen to it again, hum it, let it steep in your head, sleep with it, eat with it and be with it. After a while, your inner ear will want to hear it in your playing. Whenever you pick up the guitar and try to improvise, little nuggets of ideas will flow out without thought — the way they are or with your personal touch and expression. And trust me when I say this, all the blues giants started this way. All of them studied the greats, and their sound is a beautiful and creative amalgamation of their influences.

If you listen close enough, you can trace back any guitarist's influences — what they listened to or even what musical background they are coming from. For example, if you listen close to Stevie Ray Vaughn, you'll discover a lot of Albert King influence. But does it make him sound like Albert King?

No. Cause he ain't Albert King. He is SRV!

He "stole" those ideas and channelized them into his playing with his own touch. That's how he sounded the way he did and why no one else could. That's the path we can follow to learn and discover our own voices.

I don't consider myself a blues giant, nowhere near them. But in this chapter, I've improvised over two blues progressions and tried my best to create some memorable, musical lines over them. I've deliberately chosen to play a few licks related to concepts and techniques discussed previously in this book (or at least, a derivative of them).

In these solos, you'll discover how I go chord to chord to create connected lines without thinking about the licks. You'll observe the beat I start the phrase with and the beat I end it with. You'll notice where I pull out tasty licks from the box and how I mix it with simple melodic phrases. Take note of where and how I create tension and resolve. You'll also discover how I channel blues cliches while still being able to keep it fresh to the ear.

To help you to learn these solos exactly the way they were played, I've transcribed them. You can learn them note for note, or you can pick up a few licks or ideas. There are backing tracks for these solos in the bonus section. You can simply download it and jam along!

> Tip: Use the accompanying audio to get a full grasp of the transcribed solo.

7.1. Slow Blues in G

Guitar solo:

The first solo is a slow blues in the key of G, following a typical 12-bar blues form.

The form repeats 3 times.

2

3
19
G7
-1/2
w/bar
w/bar
w/bar
w/bar
21
D7
C7
w/bar
w/bar
23
G7
D7
25
G7
C7
G7
full
full
full
1/2
1/2
1/2

4

7.2. Shuffle blues in B

Guitar Solo:

This is relatively fast, up-tempo blues in the key of B, on a Chicago style blues shuffle groove.

A 12-bar form repeated 4 times.

2

27
E7
30
B7
let ring
let ring
33
F#7
E7
35
B7
F#7
B7
let ring
full
full
full
full
full
full
full
let ring

4
38
let ring
full
let ring
40
E7
1/2
full
43
B7
F#7
1 1/2
46
E7
B7
F#7
1 1/2

Level 8

Play With Me!

Now, we have finally come to the most fun part!

After all, you have earned it by sifting through this harmony/technique-filled bonanza of a book.

What we're gonna do here is we're gonna trade some solos!

Now, you may think, what do these Guitar Heads mean by trading solos? Is solo trade some sort of a new cryptocurrency fad? Well, carry on reading for a couple more lines and you will find out, and then you can jump right into the fun part. Sounds good? Cool.

8.1. Trading Solos

No, this is not about a new cryptocurrency fad. It is actually playing solos back and forth with another player. The idea is for us to get you up to speed so you can do this with those annoying, snobby guitar-playing friends of yours.

We're gonna do this with the solos we have shown you in the previous chapter. Use the accompanying backing tracks to jam along with us.

Solo trade No.1

Let's do the classic call and response type of thing. Our resident guitarist is going to play two bars of the shuffle blues solo in B, after which your newbie ass steps into the spotlight for another two bars, and so on...Sounds fun?

Well of course it does!

Solo trade No.2

Now that we have shook your foundations, as one shrewd Aussie once sharply remarked, let's do something a tad bit more laid back.

You go and do the first 4 bars of the solo, and let your GH instructor do the next 4 bars, and so on...We're gonna do this with the slow blues solo in G.

LEVEL 9

Gear

The irony of getting into the world of guitar gear is that it tends to become the main focus, overshadowing actual playing, for a lot of the guitar players out there. It is a bit sad once the ends become the means. However, it really is an immensely important part of your guitar playing experience. After all, the fact that tons of guitar players out there get so addicted to it just goes to show how fun and creative it is.

Since the earliest days of amplification, the tone of guitar has become much more than just the combination of right woods and nicely made fresh strings. The pickups, the pedal, the amplifier that you are using — they all make for a tone that you end up hearing.

All this can get very exciting, but maybe also somewhat intimidating. After all, we are living in the era of hyperproduction, and the number of products out there is just mind bending. Not only that, but much of the info is just sponsored stuff that doesn't take the total picture into consideration.

No worries, you have Guitar Head on your side! This is going to be a simple guide to some of the basic equipment you will be using to dial in a cool-sounding blues tone!

Sounds fun? Sure it does! Let's get right into it!

9.1. Guitar

After all, the guitar is the meat and potatoes of guitar playing, right? OK, maybe not the potatoes, but meat certainly!

The good news is, you can dial in a good blues tone on any guitar you have. It does not matter if it is a cheap Stratocaster knock-off, or a custom Gibson Les Paul, if you play your cards right, you will get a good tone.

As far as single coil pickup guitars go, Fender Stratocaster and Fender Telecaster are two guitars often associated with the genre of blues.

The pickups are literally magnets that transform the vibration of your strings into the electrical signal that is amplified by your...amplifier...How unexpected, right?

Single coil pickups offer a spanky, bright tone that is often described as glassy and twangy.

As far as the humbucker pickup equipped guitars go, the usual suspect is Gibson Les Paul.

The humbucker pickup equipped guitars produce a thicker tone with higher output than the single coil equipped guitars. The tone is often described as being fatter and warmer.

All of the aforementioned guitars are solid body guitars, meaning that there are no major holes in the wood. However, we have what we call the semi-hollow guitars which combine the solid body parts with the hollow wood body parts. One of those is the legendary Gibson ES-335. This one can be really pricey, so, if you do not have the money to afford it, DON'T WORRY. The Squire Bullet Strat will do just fine!

The most cherished thing about semi-hollow bodies is their midrange boost that blues players adore. None other than B.B. King was a keen ES-335 player for a long, long time.

9.2. Amplifiers

You know how, when unplugged, your electric guitar sounds even quieter than the acoustic guitar? Well, in order to achieve the desired loudness of your electric guitar, you need to amplify its signal first. And yes, you have guessed it — that's exactly what an amplifier does.

The pickups of your guitar pick up the vibration of your strings and transform it to an electrical signal. The electrical signal travels via your guitar cable to your amplifier. To achieve the desired increase in signal output, the amps typically use two stages: the preamp stage and the power amp stage.

The preamp stage raises the output of your guitar to a line level, and it is where most of your guitar tone is shaped. The preamp stage is where you'll typically

irish10567 from Little Falls, NJ, USA, CC BY 2.0 <https://creativecommons.org/licenses/by/2.0>, via Wikimedia Commons

find your gain and volume levels, different channels, and the EQ controls.

A lot of the amplifiers currently on the market will come with two or more different channels. At least one specialized for getting clean sounds, and at least one that has more of a distorted sound.

As far as the power amp stage goes, it takes the preamp sound and dramatically increases its level. Other than that, you can also get some tone-shaping knobs such as presence and resonance.

There are two main categories of amps: solid state and tube.

Solid state amps are usually cheaper, and they weigh much less. In comparison to the tube amplifiers, they use transistors instead of tubes to increase the signal level. Transistors never wear out or age, therefore they do not have to be replaced. Also, another advantage of the solid state amp is that it's generally less expensive than its tube counterpart.

fvancini, CC BY 2.0 <http://creativecommons.org/licenses/by/2.0>, via Wikimedia Commons

Tube amplifiers use glass valves (tubes) that are completely air free to increase the level of your guitar sound. Another important component of the tube amplifier is the transformer which matches the increased signal of the tubes to what your speaker would find most suitable in terms of level and loudness. The desirable characteristics of the tube amps are the warm sound, harmonic richness and a great dynamic response. The downside of the tube amps is that the tubes themselves are fragile and require maintenance, since the sound changes over time due to wear and tear.

There are just many, many famous amps associated with the blues genre: Fender Tweed amps, Vox AC30, Fender Deluxe Reverb, etc....

The Vox AC30 is a legendary amp that has been used by many different huge acts from various genres. It is famous for its jangly, crisp top-end sound.

Another legendary blues amp staple is the Marshall Studio Vintage SV20C. With this amp you are guaranteed a well-balanced tone. The lows are just legendary here. Clear mids and sparkling highs add up to cult status for this amp.

Some of these can get a bit pricey, but the good news is: you can dial in a great blues guitar tone even on your bedroom amp! Of course, if you are planning to gig, you would need a louder amp, but that does not take away from the tone you can get from your cheap amp.

Another example of a legendary amp is the Fender Hot Rod Deluxe. It is a combo tube amp which features a single channel with three different gain options — "clean," "drive," and "more drive."

Let's get into some basic amp setup info.

To get a good blues tone, you need to focus on the following parameters/knobs on your amp: bass, middle, treble and presence. Those are basically the EQ parameters, which means that they affect the frequencies that you will produce while playing.

Have in mind, there is no "one size fits all" recipe for dialing in a sound; on the contrary, you should experiment and come up with your original sounds. Not only that, but no two guitars are the same. Take two Squire Bullet Strats, and chances are you would need to change the amp setup between those two. Having said that, it is good to have some sort of a starting point so you can get started and try and develop your own sounds from that.

The best way to start your guitar-amp-setting journey is to put the bass, middle, treble and presence knobs on 12 o'clock.

In order to sort out your bass frequencies, play the open E chord and G barre chord. If your amp produces strange sounds and generally sounds overwhelmed, turn the bass knob down to taste. On the other hand, if those two chords sound too thin, turn up the bass knob. That's a good way to start the dialing up of your sound.

As far as treble goes, try doing this: play a really dynamic lick...Hit some notes really soft, some really hard, and everything in between. If the notes that you are hitting very hard sound ear piercing in an undesired way, turn the treble knob down.

Most of the blues guitar greats like their mid frequencies boosted. You can try and turn up your middle knob and see if you are getting those sweet sounds you like to hear from your guitar heroes.

9.3. Pedals

One of the best-known guitar pedals associated with blues guitar is the Tube Screamer.

Stevie Ray Vaughan himself used this baby boy to boost the mids of his tone and add some overdrive.

So, if you like your mids boosted and your tone a bit more gritty, this may be the way to go.

As you can see, the controls on this pedal are "drive," "tone," and "level." They were invented in order to mimic the sound of the vintage tube amp. It is a mild overdrive/distortion pedal, but it really keeps the original tone and playing prevalent as an end result.

Stevie Ray Vaughan was famous for using this pedal as a clean boost. He would put this pedal in front of the amp which was dialed to a clean channel. That way, he was able to get those incredible sharp growl attacks whenever he hit his strings hard. When he would play softly, the amp and the pedal would produce a warm, round tone.

Mataresephotos, CC BY 3.0 US <https://creativecommons.org/licenses/by/3.0/us/deed.en>, via Wikimedia Commons

Using a pedal to push your amp further and create a warm overdriven sound is a regular practice in the genre of blues. Here are some other pedal recommendations that can serve a similar purpose as a tube screamer: Boss BD-2 Blues Driver, Electro-Harmonix Nano Big Muff Pi, Boss SD-1, Super Overdrive, Electro-Harmonix Soul Food, etc...

Another legendary pedal is the Jim Dunlop Cry Baby Wah. It is a legendary piece of equipment with an even more legendary sound that a lot of the post-50s blues guitar players used and abused.

9.4. Digital Amps and Plug-Ins

After all, it is the 21st century, right?

Although we highly recommend experiencing the sheer excitement of playing your guitar through a real amp, these babies we are about to talk about can serve as wonderful substitutions/additions to your guitar arsenal.

The website, "Overload TH-U," is a library full of different amps and pedals which you can use to create some incredible sounds. The same goes for "Positive Grid Bias FX 2."

An incredibly interesting VST plugin is the Blue Cat's Re-Guitar. So, imagine you have a really cheap guitar and you would give everything you have to see how your playing would sound on a '59 Les Paul...Well, that's exactly what you can do with this incredible plug-in.

Softube Vintage Amp Room — If you want a retro-blues amp tone, look no further. This may just be the best option for you!

9.5. Fingers or Pick?

Ahh...The age-old debate!

There are definitely advantages and disadvantages to both, it really depends what you like best.

We urge you to try it out for yourself and see what you like better.

You can also look up some blues greats to see what you like better. For example, the Robert Johnson stuff is fingerpicked, while B.B. King's stuff is mostly plectrum picked. Since the skin is softer than the pick, the fingerpicking style generally produces a warmer tone with less attack, but it all comes down to the way you attack the strings and how you dial your tone.

BONUS CHAPTERS

CHAPTER 1

Minor Blues

Well guys, we have come to the end of our journey together. Well, almost. What would a Guitar Head course be without some extra stuff on the side, right?

Simply said, a minor blues is a blues in a minor key. In its most primitive form, it features minor chords throughout; however, some popular variations include dominant and major chords.

Minor blues have been used extensively throughout history, and most of the greatest blues performers have played minor blues countless times in their careers, sometimes producing famous recordings using this form.

Just like in a normal blues, a minor blues features 12 bars and the chords change place in the same spots. In other words, we start with the one chord, then go on to the fourth, back to the one and then the final four bars with the V, IV and I chords. The changes occur in the same spot as they would in a normal blues. For instance, in the key of Bm, you would play four bars of Bm and then move on to the iv chord which is Em. On bar 7, you would go back to Bm. Then on bar 9, we go to the V chord, which in this case would be F#m or F#7. The following bar goes to iv or Em. To finalize, the last two bars back on the I chord, which is Bm.

In the key of Bm, the minor blues chords are:

Bm7 | Bm7 | Bm7 | Bm7 |

Em7 | Em7 | Bm7 | Bm7 |

F#m7 | F#m7 | Bm7 | Bm7 |

In Roman numerals

---

i | i | i | i |

iv | iv | i | i |

v | v | i | i |

As you can see, the changes occur in the same exact place for both regular and minor blues. However, instead of using dominant seventh chords that are based on a major triad, the minor blues uses minor 7th chords. These are basically just a minor triad (a typical minor chord) with an added minor seventh. The addition of the minor 7th gives the minor blues a bit more of depth and a more bluesy feel than just regular minor chords.

In general terms, the minor blues have a bit more darkness to them than a regular dominant seventh chord blues. This is partly because minor chords and minor keys tend to sound more melancholic than major or dominant chords. This darkness and depth offers a very special type of flavor that has been used in countless blues songs. Bluesmen take advantage of this to express pronounced pain, and as a result, minor blues are used in countless songs — adding variety and depth to anyone's repertoire.

Minor blues are also commonly used in jazz, although not in its primitive form.

How is it different from a regular blues?

You could say that the most obvious difference between a regular blues and a minor blues is the harmony, i.e., the chords. As we've stated, the minor blues uses minor chords instead of dominant sevenths. However, music evokes feelings, and the minor blues goes well beyond just being a blues with minor chords. The overall sound and feel of a minor blues allows for the bluesman or jazzman to go to a darker place, to express emotion in a way that a regular blues may not be able to convey.

This is not to say that a minor blues is better or more heartfelt than a regular blues, but it does take the listener and performer in a more obscure direction. And this is exactly why the minor blues form has been so widely used through history. It is a vehicle to express emotion in a very unique way. And just like in a regular blues, the minor blues can be greatly varied to accommodate the composer or performer's intention and criteria. More on that later.

Notable compositions

"The Thrill Is Gone" – B.B. King: One of the greatest blues tracks of all time, unquestionably. A true blues hymn known around the world. The amount of despair that "The Thrill Is Gone" conveys is a thing a beauty, and it comes from arguably the greatest bluesman ever: the incomparable B.B. King.

"Mr. P.C." – John Coltrane: One of the many classic tracks from the seminal Giant Steps album, "Mr. P.C." is one of the most popular jazz standards around the world. Saxophone god John Coltrane plays this minor blues in a blistering-fast tempo and creates yet another one of the most popular solos in jazz.

"As The Years Go Passing By" – Albert King: Another classic minor blues song that expresses pain and suffering in an incredible way. This one is also in the key of Bm and has Albert King in full form, with his beautiful bluesy voice and incredible guitar prowess.

"Black Magic Woman" – Fleetwood Mac: This song employs a 12-bar minor blues progression, but with a few changes to spice it up a bit. Still, it uses the three chords of a minor blues progression: i, iv, v.

"Black Magic Woman" is a favorite among Fleetwood Mac fans as it evokes all that pain and emotion that are commonly found in a minor blues.

Form in B minor

The B minor key is quite popular for minor blues. Countless musicians of all styles, eras and genres have shown their prowess while playing a minor blues in Bm. This key is also favored by many guitar players, as it is relatively comfortable to in. Some of the greatest bluesmen in history have recorded minor blues in this key..

As we mentioned above, it employs the changes at the same exact spots as a regular blues, except all the chords are now minor. Because it is all minor, the Roman numerals should also reflect that. For instance, the one chord becomes "i" (as opposed to "I" from a regular blues). The "i" is still a one chord, but writing it in lowercase indicates that it is a minor chord on a minor key.

Similarly, the IV and V chords become iv and v, as they are also minor. As a result, we have a Bm blues with Roman numerals looks like this:

In Roman numerals:			
i	i	i	i
iv	iv	i	i
v	v	i	i

What can I play over the i chord?

The honest answer is that there are endless options. You can stay relatively "safe and inside" by using the most common choices for this context, or you can go all out into a realm of unfiltered expression. Here, we're going to focus on the more orthodox choices, as these will be a great place to start. Once you have mastered these obvious options, you can then start to investigate and incorporate some other choices that might not be as common, but still have a lot of value.

There are three main options of scales that you can play over the i chord. The first and most obvious is the B minor blues scale. Interestingly, you can play this scale over a regular B blues and it will also sound good. Naturally, it is tailor-made for the minor key. So much so, that you can play the B minor blues scale for the entirety of the minor blues, and it will sound good. The minor blues scale is just a minor pentatonic with an added flat 5 (the blue note). The reason the minor blues scale is the main option is that it offers that authentic blues flavor that other scales do not feature.

The second option is the B minor pentatonic scale. This one is also an obvious choice, and perhaps even easier than the B minor blues scale, as it features less notes. Additionally, the minor pentatonic is usually one of the very first scales that a guitar player learns, if not the first.

B minor pentatonic lick 1

B minor pentatonic lick 2

Finally, the third most common choice to play over the i chord is the B minor scale. The B minor scale features seven notes, so you will have more options. But remember to use your criteria wisely and pick your notes carefully. Having more notes at your disposal does not mean you have to play more notes. Playing aimlessly or without much thought is a common problem among many guitarists, and one that should be avoided.

Voice Leading: Targeting Chord tones

A good way to approach your phrases on your solos is to employ voice leading. Voice leading is using effective movement of voices (notes) from chord to chord. The strongest voice-leading choices typically involve the third and the seventh of the chord, as these are the chord tones that dictate its quality and function.

In the case of a minor blues in Bm, the first change would be from the i to the iv, or Bm to Em. For instance, the seventh of Bm (the note A) can resolve down to G (which is the third of Em). This type of movement is quite effective at outlining the harmony when improvising.

You can employ the same principle when changing from the i to the V, or Bm to F#m. For instance, here the voice leading can be from the notes D (third of Bm) up to E (seventh of F#m).

The same applies for the change from iv to i. Here you can use the third of Em (the note G) and resolve it up to the seventh of Bm (the note A).

What to play over the iv chord?

The four chord on a B minor blues is an Em. So, an E minor scale becomes an automatic option. In music, each chord has a corresponding scale, and it almost always will make sense to play it. Think of it as the same thing. After all, a minor chord is composed of the root, third and fifth of a minor scale. This, in turn, is an arpeggio. As a result, you can also play an E minor arpeggio.

Another good option to play over the iv chord is the Bm blues scale. As you become a better improviser, you will develop the intuition necessary to discern when to play what over which chord.

Em7 lick 1

Em7 lick 2 (based on the Em7 arpeggio, using chord tones)

What to play over the v chord?

The five chord on a B minor blues is a an F sharp minor. Naturally, the obvious choice here is an F# minor scale. As with the iv chord, the B minor blues scale will also work here.

It is important to note that many blues songs employ a dominant seventh chord for the five chord. In this case, you can play an F# Mixolydian scale (dominant seventh) as well as a B minor blues scale.

F#m lick 1

F#m7 lick 2 (based on the F#m triad)

F#7 dominant lick

Variations of the minor blues

The first variation of the minor blues employs a dominant seventh chord for the five, as mentioned above. The reason for substituting the F# minor for an F#7 is that the latter creates more tension. This adds depth to the minor blues, and it is the typical choice for most minor blues.

Adding a dominant seventh chord in that position is particularly effective as it also leads back to the Bm that ends the blues form.

Bm blues variation 1

Bm7 | Bm7 | Bm7 | Bm7 |

Em7 | Em7 | Bm7 | Bm7 |

F#7 | F#7 | Bm7 | F#7 |

In Roman numerals

i		i		i		i	
iv		iv		i		i	
V		V		i		V	

Another popular variation of the minor blues employs a major IV, as well as the dominant seventh on the V. In B minor, that means we have a G7 and a F#7. This variation is the de facto minor blues form for jazz and is also used by many bluesmen as it features the most dynamic movement as well as the best combination of tension and release.

Bm blues variation 2

Bm7	Bm7	Bm7	Bm7
Em7	Em7	Bm7	Bm7
G7	F#7	Bm7	F#7

In Roman numerals

i		i		i		i	
iv		iv		i		i	
V		IV		i		V	

Notable compositions

"Equinox" – John Coltrane: "Equinox" is in C# minor and features a Lydian-dominant chord on the IV. It is featured on the album Coltrane Sound and has been covered by countless musicians, often in the key of C minor, for simplicity purposes.

"Life is Hard" – Johnny Winter: A heartfelt song by the great Jonny Winter, "Life is Hard" is a minor blues in Cm that uses variations to keep it interesting and modern but at the same time follows the basic 12-bar blues form outlined above, with the IV and V chord being major.

"Black Magic Woman" – Fleetwood Mac: This classic rock track is actually a blues in D minor. It features a unique variation where the order of some chords is slightly changed. A fantastic example of a minor blues form in a rock context.

"Birk's Works" – Dizzy Gillespie: This minor blues composed by trumpet extraordinaire Dizzy Gillespie features several ii V additions for a special jazz flavor. "Birk's Works" is a standard, and still often played and taught all over the world.

Conclusion

The minor blues features the same form of a blues but with minor chords. Often, variations adding dominant chords on the IV and V are employed, to increase dramatic effect and tension. The minor blues offers a unique avenue of expression as it is a blues but with a darker and edgier overall quality.

Some of the best-known blues songs are minor blues, especially in jazz, where this form is must-know for musicians all over the world. Minor blues can also be used in a rock context and the blues scale of the corresponding key can be employed quite over the entire progression.

So, take the time to learn some minor blues, in their primitive form as well as at least the two main variations which incorporate dominant chords on the IV and V. From a learning perspective, is not much different than a regular blues, as it features 12 bars and the chords change in the same positions.

CHAPTER 2

Advanced Chords

This chapter goes beyond the newbie scope and takes you into some advanced territories. The more advanced stuff we are about to show you is generally in regards to rhythmic and harmonic vocabulary you currently possess.

So, what we're gonna do is we're gonna show you five different variations of the basic 12-bar blues chord progression in G.

Before we jump in, let's just cover the chords we are going to use:

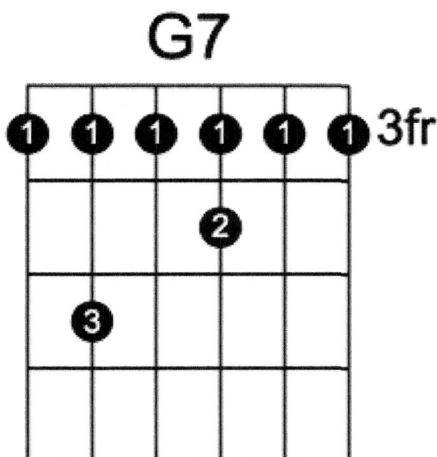

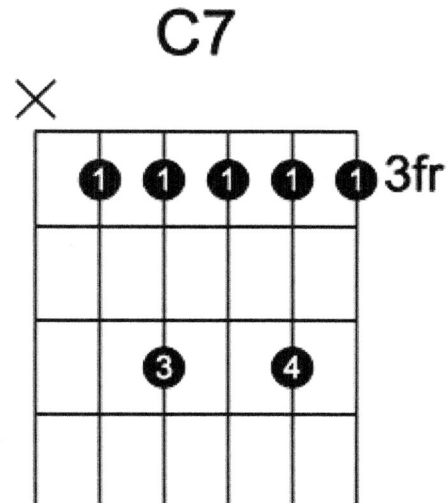

G7

C7

D7

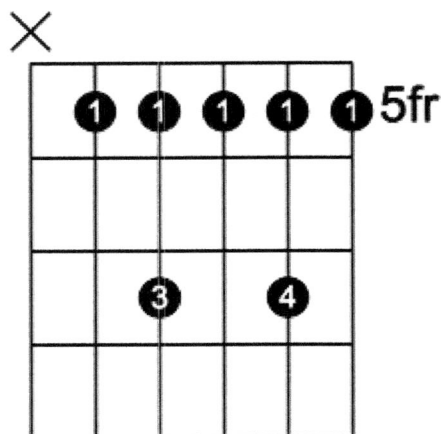

Am7

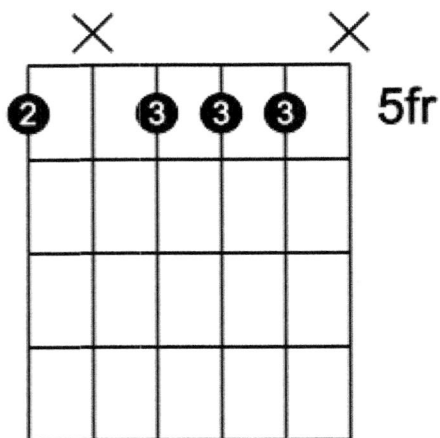

E7

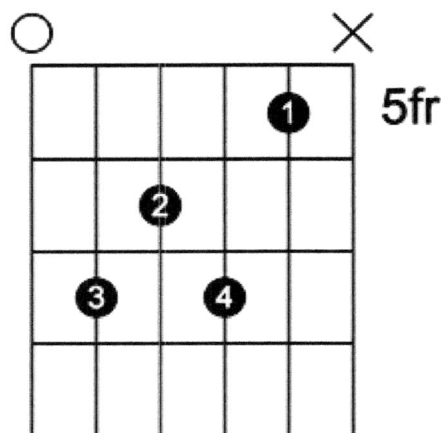

Db°7

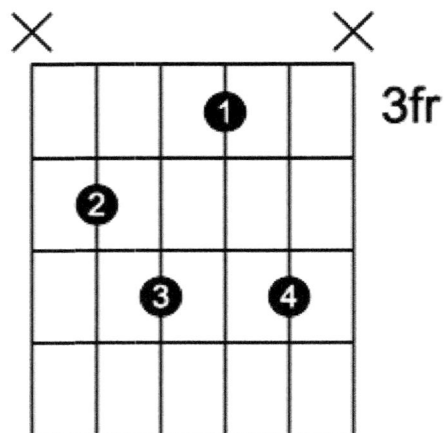

A7

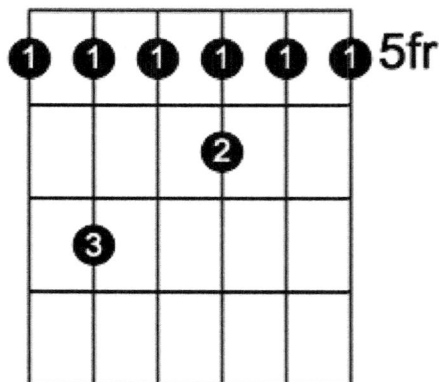

Advanced Progression No.1:

Substituting chords in a blues progression is a common practice among blues and jazz musicians. This way you can create 'harmonic motion' to the progression and keep it interesting.

Even if a soloist is playing blues cliches, these kinda variations add a new level to the comping. You can feed a soloist these chords and keep the progression fresh and different.

You can see in bar 2, I have substituted the I chord with the IV chord. It's played only for one bar before resolving to I chord again. Playing A7 for 4 bars could be monotonous for some of us. Throwing IV into the mix adds a bit of harmonic movement to the progression.

As far as the strumming pattern goes, try it like this: up, up, down, up. Repeat that for every bar. Also, do not bother to hit all the strings all the time, since that will make it sound too robotic. This should be very feel-based. When you hit down, you will probably leave out some high strings; the same goes for hitting the upstroke and leaving out some low strings. Don't worry, it is a more desirable sound anyway —a real groovy feeling

Advanced Progression No. 2

Watch out for bar 9! V chord has been substituted by IIm. It is also a companion minor of D7, thus creating a II-V- I move in the progression. FYI, I say II-V-I is the meat and the potato of most jazz songs.

Substituting V7 with IIm is a common practice in jazz tradition.

As far as the strumming pattern goes, try it like this: down, down, up, down, up, down, up. Repeat that for every bar.

Advanced Progression No.3

As far as the strumming pattern goes, try it like this: down, up, up, up, up. Repeat that for every bar.

Harmonically, there are two significant changes here. First, on bar 8 we substitute I chord with the VI7 (E7). Why? E7 is the V chord of the Am7. And it resolves nicely on Am7. As we know, going V to I creates a perfect cadence.

For the same reason, we use D7 on bar 12. D7 is the V of G7, and it ends the cycle and resolves to the G7 beautifully.

Advanced Progression No.4:

On bar 6, we have introduced a concept called dominant-diminished substitution. A dominant chord and a diminished chord a half step above it, share almost all same note.

In this case, lets compare the C7 and Db diminished 7, which is half step above C7.

We know C7 is made of C, E, G and Bb.

And Db diminished 7th has Db, G, Bb and E.

Apart from one note, they have the same notes.

You can always substitute a dominant chord by a diminished 7th chord up a half step.

But remember: Diminished 7th chord has a tense sound, so it needs to be resolved. And we resolved the Db diminished 7th to G7 as a tritone substitution.

As far as the strumming pattern goes, try it like this: down, up. Repeat that for every bar.

Advanced Progression No.5:

This progression has classic I-VI-II-V turnaround. We have discussed the 1625 turnaround in chapter 5. This is another common tool for jazz musicians.

Yes, with this you can jazzify your progression.

As far as the strumming pattern goes, try it like this: down, down, up, down. Repeat that for every bar.

Conclusion

We hope you have enjoyed this ride, cause we certainly did. It is always an incredible feeling to help someone understand the blues since it is the music form that helped revolutionize the music as we know today. The clash of the African musical heritage with the modern Westernized instrumentation left the world of music forever changed and opened up once unimaginable frontiers in terms of harmony, performance, instrumentation and literally everything else. Basically, to understand modern music, you must understand the blues. Even more importantly, the electric guitar playing style was predominantly developed either by blues players, or the players heavily influenced by blues. When it first appeared on the scene, the blues was so revolutionary and irresistible that it immediately influenced a whole host of different genres. Nowadays, the blues influence is so ingrained in so many different genres, that it is hard to think that it came from somewhere else. Newer generations tend to think of the blues as a conservative art form, which it is today, to a certain extent. But once it appeared it broke so many boundaries, that it is really hard to grasp from our modern-day viewpoint. Nevertheless, understanding the process of development of blues can do wonders for your own creativity. After all, to create real art you must not imitate the final product, you should imitate the process. Still, there are some areas in which blues has been unsurpassed ever since. Mainly, it is the phrasing and the feel. Which is literally the mother of all soulful guitar playing, no matter what genre you like. We certainly hope we have kickstarted that journey for you in a respectful way to you as a reader, as well as in a respectful way to the ever-inspiring art form which is the blues!

Until next time, let your guitar do all the talking from the deepest depths of your soul! After all, there's no better framework for that than its majesty - the blues!

Farewell

Pssssstttt....

What are you doing here? Are you lost?

Do people even look at the last pages of a book?

Jokes aside, I hope you enjoyed this book. I certainly loved the process of writing it.

If you enjoyed this book, could you take 2 minutes to leave a review about it?

Reviews are the lifeblood for small publishers and help us get our books into the hands of more guitarists like you.

We read every review personally and appreciate each one of it.

To leave a review, simply go to the platform you purchased the book from and type in your review.

With that said, here's Guitar Head signing off!

Until next time then? I'll see you in another book.

THE END

Guitar Notation

OK, before you get overwhelmed by the weird diagrams below, let me explain.

Guitar tablature has more to it than just strings and fret numbers. You might have come across some strange signs and symbols while learning your licks or exercises. We call them notation legends.

Here we have listed some of them you often bump into.

HAMMER-ON:
Pick the lower note first, then hit the second note with a finger of left hand without picking.

PULL-OFF:
Pick the higher note first, then pull the finger off to sound the second note. Make sure both fingers are placed at the same time before the first hit

PTHRILL:
Pick the first note and alternate rapidly between that note and the one in brackets using hammer-ons and pull-offs.

LEGATO SLIDE:
Pick the first note and, using the same finger, slide through the fretboard until next note. Don't struck the next note

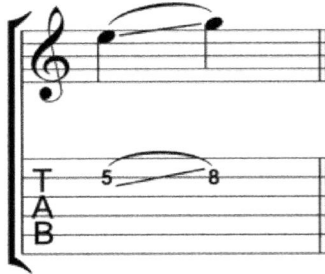

SLIDE:
Pick the first note and, using the same finger, slide through the fretboard until next note. The next

VIBRATO: With the fretting hand vibrate the string up and down using small bends and releases. Exaggerate the effect to create a wide vibrato.

TAPPING: With a finger of the pick hand hammer-on the note indicated with + sign (T on the tab) and then pull-off to the lower note fretted by the fret hand.

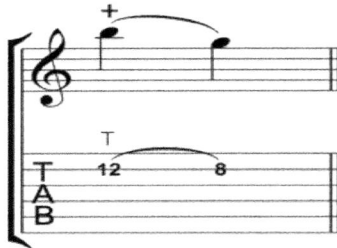

PALM MUTING:
Place the side of the palm of the pick hand right before the bridge to touch lightly the string(s) and produce a muted sound.

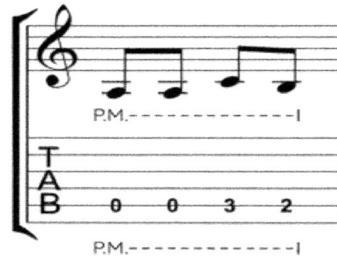

MUFFLED STRINGS:
Place the fret hand across the strings with a slightly touch (without pressing the strings against the fret), strum with the pick hand to produce a percussive sound.

WHOLE-STEP BEND:
Pick the note and then bend up a whole tone.

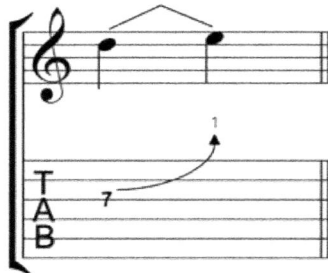

HALF-STEP BEND:
Pick the note and then bend up a half tone.

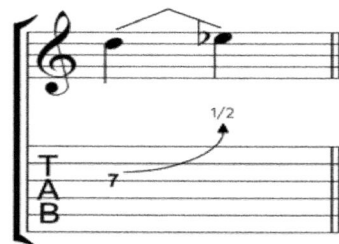

QUARTER-TONE BEND:
Pick the note and then bend up a quarter-tone

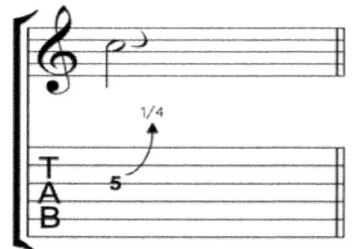

BEND AND RELEASE:
Pick the note, bend the amount indicated and then release the bend to the first note.

GRACE NOTE BEND:
Pick the note, and bend the amount indicated immediately.

PRE-BEND:
First bend the string the amount indicated and then strike the string.

PRE-BEND & RELEASE:
First bend the string the amount indicated, strike the string and then release the bend.

NATURAL HARMONIC:
Play the note placing the fret hand finger lightly over the string directly at the fret indicated and releasing the finger after the note starts to ring.

WHAMMY BAR SCOOP:
Press down the bar just before striking the note and then release the push returning the bar to original place.

PINCH HARMONIC:
Place the fret hand finger normally and with the pick hand, strike the note normally and at the same time the edge of the thumb has to make contact with the string.

ARTIFICIAL HARMONIC:
Fret the note normally, then lightly place your index finger directly over the fret indicated in parenthesis, then pick the note with your thumb or ring finger.

WHAMMY BAR DIVE AND RETURN: Play the note, then, push down the bar to produce the pitch indicated with the number and finally release the push returning bar to original place.

There are many more notation legends to extend this list. We could fill up a book talking about it all. But these are good to go. If you want to explore tabs in detail, I have a free book on guitar tabs.

You can go download it here: theguitarhead.com/tabs

Printed in Great Britain
by Amazon

86785792R00086